INTERSTATE COMMERCE

INTERSTATE COMMERCE

REGIONAL STYLES OF DOING BUSINESS

CLYDE W. BURLESON

A GROLIER COMPANY

1987   FRANKLIN WATTS   NEW YORK

Library of Congress Cataloging-in-Publication Data

Burleson, Clyde W.
  Interstate commerce.

  Includes index.
   1. Business etiquette—United States.
2. Regionalism—United States.   3. Interstate
commerce.   I. Title.
HF5387.B856 1987 381'.5'0973 86-29019
ISBN 0-531-15519-6

CONTENTS

PREFACE

People in different parts of America live differently. That's a simple, often overlooked fact.

People in different parts of America also work differently, have different customs and manners, speak differently, and respond differently to certain social stimuli.

When you leave your office and fly a thousand miles to do business with someone from another region of the U.S., you confront those differences. As you do when telephoning a person across the country or greeting an out-of-town counterpart.

Understanding regional differences will make you a better manager. A more successful one, too, because understanding why a person reacts in a seemingly unexpected manner, or responds sharply to an apparently innocuous comment, allows you to control the situation and avoid misunderstandings.

A basic business tenet holds that all parties in a deal should have a clear concept of precisely what their gains will be. "What's in it for me?" is a powerful question.

In this book, what's in it for you is knowledge about others and about yourself, too. Your use of that knowledge will allow you to get more from your efforts at *interstate commerce.*

From knowledge comes understanding. From understanding, success. That's what this book is really about: enhancing your success when you conduct business with those who live and work in other parts of America.

INTERSTATE COMMERCE

CHAPTER

1

PAPER MIRROR

Regional differences really exist.

In the beginning, it looked like one of those once-in-a-career opportunities: an investment sweet enough to make everyone say, "How much will we make?" as opposed to "Can we make it work?"

Experience indicates that if a deal looks too good to be true, it probably is. In this case, the price of oil plummeted and all promise of profit dissolved like a paper airplane in a hailstorm. The situation went from satisfied thoughts of money in the bank to near-distress loss cutting.

There was only one minor matter still unresolved. How much would each player lose?

The attorneys suggested a meeting, so the partners gathered. Who would stand by their commitments? And if one wavered, would the rest panic and run?

It was, to say the least, a tense situation. The investors were emotionally charged. No one in the group had ever seen any of the others because there had been no face-to-face contact. All business had been conducted by letter or brief telephone exchanges. Every member of this amalgam of strangers represented interests from "back home," and "back home" was a different part of the country for each participant.

The conference convened promptly at ten on a fine spring morning. At that moment, attendees got a first look at the other partners. Influenced by regional bias and stereotypes, they formed their first impressions.

Stereotypes do not reflect any one person, but rather the general perception of a group. Applying a stereotype to any single individual may be inaccurate. Yet there is a lot of truth in the stereotype, or it wouldn't have stayed with us long enough to enter our folklore.

Not all Yankee shopkeepers are sharp-nosed, economical with their words, and peer over the top of rimless glasses. Not all bankers are fat. Many Las Vegas party-goers do not dress in open-neck white silk shirts adorned with gold chains. Many Texas oil magnates do not possess a pair of cowboy boots, or prefer a Stetson to a homburg. Many New York business executives speak slowly and calmly. Many Los Angeles talent agents wear three-piece suits.

Then again, enough in each case do the opposite, giving birth to the stereotype which, in turn, gives an emotional feeling, right or wrong, about those from the characterized locale.

The New Yorker at this meeting sat next to a Virginian, who was mistrustful of his colleague, believing the New Yorker's own, well-publicized credo that "If you make it in New York, you can make it anywhere." The Virginian was convinced he was dealing with a slick customer, an ultimate sophisticate to whom business was as much a game of wits as a matter of money. Mindful of his Southern feeling that a New Yorker would rather outsmart you and make a nickel than do a straight deal and earn a dime, the Virginian took a tight mental grip on his bank account.

The New Yorker was ready for the slow, mush-mouthed circumlocution he was certain the Virginian was about to deliver. The Southerner would probably do the right thing, ultimately, but only after endless explaining and re-explaining and a final invoking of that power-beyond-all-powers, the matter of Honor.

As for the Texan across the table, the New Yorker felt personal distaste. When that loudmouth started gabbing, there would be no shutting him up. Texans always talked. Big and long. The Virginian, looking at the same person, saw an ally, one to whom doing right would matter more than the money. Although the money mattered, of course.

The attendee who annoyed the New Yorker was a Los Angeleno. Sunny California baked shrewdness into their brains. All smiles and "Baby, you're beautiful," they would clip you hard enough to hurt anytime they could make a buck.

The Los Angeles investment advisor returned the compliment. Those New York shysters were as good as their word, which wasn't any good at all.

The lady from Chicago was leery of the New Yorker. And the clown from Los Angeles. The Southerner was all right. So was the Texan—a little brash, but okay. The lawyer from Davenport, Iowa, was reliable, too. She vowed to watch the coastal contingent to see that they took their medicine like all the rest, without sneaking any special benefits. Then there was the Latin type from Miami. Charming, but unquestionably devious.

And so it went. Each sized up the other, using stereotypes, personal bias, and past experience.

Even after the meeting advanced and participants had an opportunity to verbalize their positions, preconceived stereotypes remained in minds, shading the meaning of the speaker's words.

The outcome was predictable. And equitable. Some felt they might have gained a greater advantage by one act or another, but the deal had been carefully developed before the investment had been made and the attorneys did their homework.

The attendees emerged from the session somewhat poorer financially, but a little richer intellectually. Their recall of stereotypes had provided each with a feeling about the others. This was, in turn, modified by individual behavior during the meeting. The result was a quicker, more intense understanding of positions and, from that, a more rapid accord through the give-and-take of compromise.

The Virginian, who hadn't been quite as slow as the New Yorker dreaded, found an ally in the Texan, but the Chicagoan had been helpful, too. And the Los Angeles whiz hadn't tried to dominate the session with mirrors and smoke.

There's a moral to this simple story. It's made in two points. First, as everyone present learned again, business is more than a shuffling of papers, a moving of goods, the making of a deal, or the counting of money. Business is a matter of people. And in business, people matter. Second, people from different regions of the United States differ from each other.

Part of knowing about people is to recognize that environment plays a role in shaping our actions, attitudes, manners, and behavior. Since America is a large nation, a number of substantially different environments exist side by side. Business people who come from these diverse places will have different characteristics. Of course, they share similarities, too. But there are notable differences.

Many ways of measuring the likenesses and differences in people from various geographic areas have been developed. One of the most interesting is the study of cultural geography.

Cultural geographers make it their business to study regional differences in America. They have divided our nation based on any criteria that sound interesting, producing maps tracing routes taken by touring country and western music groups, locations of pizza parlors in eastern Pennsylvania, and the disposition of individuals with any of sixteen unusual surnames throughout South Dakota.

They've also singled out birth rates, death rates, access to medical care, numbers of school dropouts, percentage of population graduating from college, low incomes, high incomes, medium incomes, no incomes, percentage of population on the Federal dole, and thousands of other useful or useless definitions as parameters for splitting America.

Somehow, during all this activity, those who made it their business to divide and subdivide did not direct attention to the world of business. More specifically, business executives.

Why cultural geographers didn't get around to this, no one seems to know. The subject is immensely more interesting than knowledge of which parts of the country use fake yak-hide floor coverings or the purchasing patterns of condoms against incidence of IUD for birth control.

Possibly, cultural geographers have made it their business to leave business executives alone because they are hard to study. Hard, but hardly impossible.

A great deal of information has been collected for this book.

Want a sample?

How much small talk is appropriate before a meeting in various parts of the U.S.? What are appropriate or inappropriate subjects? (There are areas where topics covered during the ice-breaking or warm-up portion of a conference or phone conversation never focus on family or personal matters. In other locales, not to ask about family members shows a lack of concern and poor taste.)

Is there a difference in elevator etiquette?

Or parking lot protocol?

What about drinking at noon? Or drinking any time?

Or the use of profanity in the office? It's acceptable, to varying degrees, in certain areas.

Consider different interpretations given to the same statement. The language doesn't change, but the meaning can.

And dress. If a banker in New York buys a suit identical in brand, color, and style to suits bought by bankers in Dallas and San Francisco, will all three be look-alikes? (The answer is "no" because of regional variations in fit, accessories, belts, ties, tie length after knotting, and the manner in which the suit is worn. People do wear clothes differently in different regions. Shoes and socks selected to go with the suit are another variation, as are hair styles.)

The list goes on and on.

How critical are the differences? Are they serious enough to break a deal? Not usually, although they have. Strong enough to hurt feelings or cause unpleasantness? You bet.

Try this true tale as an example:

A Chicago executive flew to Dallas. When he returned home, he wasn't mad, he was livid. Calling a friend who lived in Houston, he was angry enough to cut short the mandatory Chicago small talk. (Which, by the way, is known as an "opening amenity" among people who classify this kind of data. Chicago opening amenities are shorter than those used in Dallas and Houston and are less family-oriented than those common in Texas.)

The gist of his problem, based on his latest experience, was that Texans, specifically those he met in Dallas, were insincere phonies—not able to be taken at their word. They would do anything to make a deal.

During negotiations, all participants were congenial. When the transaction was complete, though, the Texas boys gave him the cold shoulder. This showed, as far as the Chicagoan was concerned, their insincerity.

The basis for the misunderstanding, because that's what it was, came down to a regional expression/custom.

Before the sale, one of the Texans said, "After we get this deal over, let's get together for dinner one night." The Chicagoan took the remark as an actual invitation, a clear statement of intent. Later, when he tried to set a date, he got evasion and a queer look.

The Texan said it, but only as a pleasantry. A "Why don't we do so-and-so" class of remark is intended as a "How are you?" (In Texas, that comes out "Hey! How you?") Acceptance of the "invitation" is viewed with the same disbelief and disenchantment as if someone, in reply to "How are you?", answered with an endless litany of problems, medical woes, marital upsets, and financial disasters.

The response was simply out of character with the thought behind the comment.

In Dallas, Houston, and San Antonio—three cities with distinct regional attitudes, by the way—a sincerely extended invitation is highly specific, along the lines of "Why don't we get together Thursday night for dinner at my place." (Note the absence of a question mark. That's because it's said as a statement, not a question. Another regional quirk.)

The Chicagoan was appeased when he discovered the different meanings of the same sentence. He was also a little disturbed by how he'd appeared to his Texas partner. The situation didn't kill a deal, but unresolved it would certainly have made further dealings less pleasant.

Another Southern and Western custom causes misunderstandings on a more frequent basis. A popular phrase, spoken as customers leave restaurants and retail establishments, is "Ya all come back now! Hear?" "Hear" is pronounced "hee-ah." Two syllables.

Many visitors from outside the region, hearing this friendly admonition as they reach the door, and believing the statement to be a command, turn and obey instructions. That is, they come back, only to confront a shopkeeper or cashier who is looking at them oddly. A silence usually ensues as each person awaits the other's next move. The visitor stands, wondering why he/she was loudly, and some feel rudely, stopped from going about his/her business. The retail person has no idea why the individual standing there has returned, but is willing to wait to find out. It's funny to watch it happen, especially if you know what caused the contretemps.

A final example concerns three executives from Los Angeles, two men and a woman, who went to Knoxville on a matter relating to the world exposition held in the city a few years ago.

The purpose of the meeting was to finalize an agreement dealing with the manufacture and sale of a number of novelties (T-shirts, pennants, ashtrays, etc.) bearing pictures and theme slogans of the fair. ("Finalize," by the by, is a Los Angeles word now used in most of the U.S., meaning to "make final" or "complete." It stands as an example of regional business speech that has spread. The main source today for such jargon is no longer Los Angeles but Washington, D.C.)

Arriving at the meeting, the West Coast team was ushered into a conference room. After the normal "You all care for some coffee?" and everyone was settled, the Los Angeles group opened their presentation along these lines:

"Based on the attendance estimates you supplied and our past experience with the various items, you've got a gold mine. We call the profit a very cool million seven, and your group keeps half. With no responsibility for the unsold merchandise. What doesn't move, we take back! A mil seven in American, green, U.S. of A. dollars. That's what we ought to clear, easy. A million seven split between us!" As he spoke, he wrote the figure $1,700,000.00 on a chalk board so everyone could see the magic number.

The effect on the room was not what was expected. The Knoxvillians looked pained, looked at each other, looked away, and looked embarrassed.

Seeing the reaction, and thinking the amount wasn't sufficient or was below their expectations, the Californian pressed on, telling them the million seven was only an estimate and the income might go as high as two million.

The more he talked, the more he could see his words were only making things worse. Following his instincts, he closed his mouth and motioned to his associate, who gave her part of the presentation focusing on the items, their uniqueness, and the quality of workmanship. The Knoxville group brightened considerably and followed her with growing enthusiasm.

The third member of the Los Angeles team also received interest and attention during his discussion of the system for defining optimum locations for sales outlets.

The leader, in his selling close, again focused on profits and, to his dismay, saw the audience again fidget and appear uncomfortable.

Everyone was cordial at the end of the meeting and, after reasonable adjournment amenities, parted.

The Los Angeles group did not get the order. In trying to discover why, the second presenter talked to one of the female executives on the buyer's side. The response was straightforward, but mysterious.

"It was obvious to all of us you know your business," the woman said, "but it was also clear we'd never get along with your boss. He's way too rude and pushy for us down here." More probing finally led to an answer in terms the Los Angeles group could comprehend.

Discussion of profits to be taken from a deal is a matter of regional variance. In Los Angeles, it is good form to plunge in and plug away at the subject. In the South, profits are taken for granted, but never, repeat never, publicly discussed. Mentioned, fine. Alluded to, great. Shown in detail on an operating summary sheet, necessary. But discussed? No. Made the opening feature and main point of a presentation? Never, never, never.

To the Southerners, the Los Angeles team leader's performance was barbaric. It appeared to them profit was his sole motive—the only part of the transaction he cared about. This created an impassable barrier. Each member of the Knoxville group could imagine all future discussion tinged by the specter of money. Worse, they could foresee endless arguments and awkward confrontations over money, a subject they hesitated to discuss with good friends in the best of circumstances.

Focusing on the wrong element turned an otherwise effective presentation into a shambles. Both wanted profits, but one side had regional limitations on discussing such matters.

It's a little thing, but it made a big difference. Did it ruin the deal? Who can say? The Los Angeles firm might not have gotten the business in any case. There is no question, though, that not understanding local custom harmed their chances.

Regional differences in the conduct of business and the manners and behavior of business executives exist. They can exert a profound effect on negotiations between individuals from different areas of the U.S. Understanding these variations will allow you to anticipate problems and turn them to your best advantage. Use this book like a paper mirror—to see yourself as others perceive you, before they even say "hello."

CHAPTER

2

DIVIDING
AMERICA

Define the differences,
then the regions
define themselves.

Cultural geographers don't divide America. They allow America to divide itself each time they analyze the U.S. for areas of common traits. And while, like professors in every field, they have their little spats, there is almost unanimous agreement on certain boundaries.

One recognized segment stems from sides chosen by various states during our late, lamented civil disturbance. "Lamented" is a questionable word, in this case, because the only lament a sizable portion of the Southern population has is losing what they still feel was "their" war.

"The South," both words capitalized, is a phrase which defines a specific area of the country to any business person. There may be some argument about borderline states, but generally, if one business executive says: "Our market is mostly in the South," the communication is clear.

Another accepted split, also stemming from a historical base, is "The West," to which, in the mid-1800s, John Soule and Horace Greeley, in separate pieces of business advice to those junior in years, urged young adults to go. Actually, they urged only young male adults. In their day, young women were better left at home.

Greeley's "West" was Kansas or Nebraska, two states not deemed western to anyone raised on Hollywood cowboy films of the 1940s or '50s. Today, "The West" applies to states closer to the Pacific.

To discuss regional variations in business behavior, there first must be defined regions. That's the task of this chapter.

For this book, a cut-and-fit process was created, based on various fudge factors, because it was impossible to always divide along state boundaries. Eastern and western New York state is one example. Then there is Texas, which for years preserved the right to split itself into five separate states.

Interestingly, divisions settled upon to demonstrate regional variations in business behavior match many of those based on other criteria. This leads to the idea that maybe, just maybe, differences can be the result of common social experience. And that common experience influences attitudes.

At any rate, beginning in the northeast and moving across America, here are the major areas of the U.S. in which business managers and executives reflect distinct regional differentiation.

CONSERVATORY *(Maine, New Hampshire, Vermont, Massachusetts, Connecticut, Rhode Island)*

Six New England states form a natural cluster on a map. They stand alone. From the rocky Maine coastline south to parts of Connecticut, more connected with Manhattan than with the rest of the world, there are variations. But these are far outweighed by similarities.

There is a clear consistency in the dress, manners, and behavior of the management class. And clearly, major differences exist between this group and their New York friends, not to mention those with their Los Angeles counterparts.

One city in the area has made itself an American legend. Boston exudes its own aura. In some ways, executives in Boston have taken the strongest aspects of New England's plentiful biases and intensified them dramatically. At the same time, other area attitudes have been disclaimed. Boston is unique. A zone of eupeptic eccentricities.

Questions that produced a uniform response from the balance of New England received a different reception in Boston. So a new term had to be developed to indicate our six New England states with Boston as a separate entity. Hence, the CONSERVATORY, a reference to the segment of the U.S. where tradition moderates forces which show more power in other parts of the nation. In this unusual piece of America, even factors of profit and loss are dampened by tradition-dominated management concepts. In the CONSERVATORY, it's bad to lose money, but worse to make it in the wrong style.

COMMERCIAL CORRIDOR   *(Eastern New York, eastern Pennsylvania, a portion of New Jersey, and Delaware)*

The eastern border of New York state is an almost vertical line on maps. From there, south and west, through Pennsylvania, New Jersey, and Washington, D.C., is a densely populated COMMERCIAL CORRIDOR which exerts tremendous influence on commerce in America and the world. The western portions of New York and Pennsylvania, along Lakes Ontario and Erie, belong to another district. The balance of the zone is dominated by New York City, especially Manhattan, and Philadelphia. These two different urban centers are surrounded by a surprisingly homogeneous business population.

On a square mile basis, this is a small geographic unit. From the standpoint of business, it is huge. The impact of decisions made here are felt across the nation.

Please notice that Washington, D.C. is excluded from the COMMERCIAL CORRIDOR. Washington, D.C. is excluded from the rest of America, too. There are other big cities in the world which equal New York as a business capital. These are usually national seats of government, as well. There is no city in the world which can be paired with Washington, D.C. It's a beginning and an end, all alone. In addition to being a hodgepodge of customs, it has only one focus. Government affairs. Take away the government, and no one would choose life in the half-swamp, semi-tidal flat which makes up much of the central city's land area.

Business people in other regions look at New York City with a mixture of awe and revulsion. New Yorkers sum up their attitude in a single, often repeated statement: "If you can make it in New York, you can make it anywhere."

Individuals from other parts of the nation debate the veracity of that comment. And note that the very traits New Yorkers single out for success are not so grandly appreciated elsewhere. There is a strong argument that not even New Yorkers appreciate those traits to the degree in which they are used in doing business in Manhattan. Nonetheless, the theory reflects a distinct New York bias. An unspoken corollary is clear: "If you haven't made it here, as far as I'm concerned, you haven't made it. No matter how successful you were back in Podunk."

This thought process also is resented by a majority of non-New Yorkers. That resentment is recognized by New Yorkers. The philosophy as espoused in the two sentences contains the true path to glory in Apple City.

In one word, it is "survival." Living in New York City is so difficult, as compared to almost anywhere else in the United States, just muddling through another day requires real effort. If a business person can survive, and at the same time contribute to an organization's growth or success, that certainly is an achievement.

Arnold Toynbee, the historian, spoke to the challenge he termed "Hard Lands." Polynesians were an island group which never developed what he defined as a true culture. The challenge from their bountiful lands was slight; living demanded too little of humankind, so the imperative to grow into a culture was nonexistent. Eskimos, on the other hand, failed to develop a true culture because their challenge was too great. Every waking moment was given to pure survival. There was no time or energy left to produce a culture.

The hardness of New York City, as a land, must be about right. For those who can survive and have time remaining to devote to careers and business, rewards are worthy of the game.

Philadelphia is also a hard land of about the correct degree of difficulty. The city is an awkward size with a "big town/small town" enigma. It is large enough to offer mega-measures of inconvenience, yet there is little more than a minimum dollop of ambiance in compensation. Arts are present but in insufficient amounts; culture is at levels far below New York; and an indecent number of middle-grade restaurants turn out mediocre food, serve it badly, and charge as if it were grand. The "Philly cheese steak," a sandwich, has spread from coast to coast, and aside from the Liberty Bell, Cream Cheese, and the Phillies, this is the town's only claim to national fame.

Regardless of the role of politics, much of the city's direction is controlled by an established old guard which considers second generation Philadelphians newcomers and reveres tradition to the point of making it a secular religion. The impact of entrenched hierarchy has been immune to time. This directly affects business life and, if it weren't for custom and habit, managements would depart, leaving the area to blue-collar workers. That, as a consequence, would move the majority of Pennsylvania out of the COMMERCIAL CORRIDOR into the adjacent industrial zone.

No one in Philadelphia says, "If you make it here, you

can make it anywhere." First, because making it in Philly isn't like making it anywhere else. And secondly, New Yorkers would laugh scornfully, the fear of which gives Philadelphians an intense, and possibly well-deserved, inferiority complex.

THE SOUTHLANDS *(Maryland, Virginia, North and South Carolina, Georgia, Florida, Alabama, Mississippi, Louisiana, eastern Texas, Tennessee, Arkansas, and a segment of Kentucky)*

As a term, "South" is no longer functional. The former sons and daughters of the Confederacy have subdivided. Some claim "Yankee" influence has finally taken toll. In reality, there never was a single "South." There have always been three distinct areas—four, if Texas is included because of the arid, far western reaches of the state. Three, though, is enough to compartmentalize today's business community. Most of Texas will be inserted elsewhere.

The Atlantic Coastal South extends from the Maryland state line to Miami. In this unending stretch of Atlantic shore, the Coastal South is dominant. Aside from Washington, D.C. (that anomaly in any effort to classify America), major cities hardly differ from a business standpoint. Names and power groups change, accents vary, but attitudes, manners, and dress are much the same.

Question: What is unusual about Richmond, Virginia; Raleigh, North Carolina; Charleston, South Carolina; Savannah, Georgia; Jacksonville, Florida; and other urban centers in this zone? What do they have in common?

Answer: Business customs and behavior in these "big" cities are much like those displayed in the region's smaller cities. In fact, even including the balance of the traditional "South," no other place in America comes close to this level of unanimity in urban, suburban, and rural business conduct.

Why do urban business executives think and act much like their country cousins? Because these major centers are populated with business people who by and large grew up in smaller towns and, at the end of their formal education, moved to the vibrant, bigger city, seeking more opportunity. This in-migration has, at least to date, been a strong unifying force, leveling variations between urban and rural forces.

This Atlantic Coastal South has another unique feature: the sharing of American colonial traditions with the CON-SERVATORY. This commonality is seen in similarities of response between the two regions on many questions. Both share a love-hate relationship with our founding fathers and exercise a traditional mistrust of each other based on commercial values of the 1700s. Yet both are proud lands, where Colonial America took root. In several ways, they are more alike under their facades than one would, from appearances, suppose.

The Inland South/Gulf South are two distinct regions which, along their joining line, blend together. At the extreme edges, there is significant difference. Where they touch, they take on the appearance of the Inland South.

Colonial tradition is nonexistent, as are emotional ties to an England of a bygone age.

Inland South is a traditionally southern zone bounded by a ring of cities with almost northern character. The area, defined by connecting Richmond, Louisville, Little Rock, Birmingham, and Atlanta into a blimp-shaped territory, shows similarities to another area, covered later, edging the Great Lakes.

The Inland South provides manufacturing and commercial services for the entire southeastern quadrant of the United States. And does it amid endless chains of hills and rounded mountains, populated by hard-case, isolated agrarians who carry individual freedom and chauvinism to extremes unequaled in other regions.

Atlanta is the skew city in this zone, different from its compatriots, companion to none. Three distinct business clusters, including the Atlantic Center with its copper-roofed tower, the so-called Midtown, and the older downtown, prove the point. More business is conducted here than in all other cities in the region combined. In Atlanta, another factor has been added to the in-migration of southern, smaller-town success seekers.

As a regional transportation center since the early 1820s, Atlanta has always enjoyed an occupation by "outsiders." Originally, anyone from more than a few miles away was considered an "outsider." That conservative thought process still lingers, but has given way under an influx of business types who share a more sophisticated world view.

Atlanta considers itself cosmopolitan. Compared to Salt Lake City, in many ways it is. Compared to New York, or Boston, or San Francisco, or even Houston, it is not.

For years, business community "insiders" and "outsiders" conflicted on virtually every issue. As soon, however, as there was enough money for all, Atlantans settled their disputes and prospered. Today, yesterday's outsiders resist new arrivals. It's a story played so often as to become legend.

In the best legendary style, business-oriented Atlantans ignore the problem and go their own way. And their way is different: in style of speech, dress, manners, and habits.

To sum up Atlanta in one statement: It is the only city in the South in which the business community has more in common with associates in Dallas or New York than smaller southern towns. The place is a border marker between the Gulf and Inland South, vital to each, catering to each and, to some degree, controlling each.

Birmingham, Chattanooga, Louisville, with its access to the Ohio River, Memphis, Little Rock, and other cities in the Inland South exist as factories and transfer points.

Tampa, Mobile, Biloxi, and scattered population centers

along the Gulf of Mexico are different. Southern in their dress, manners, and speech, the business cadre of the "third coast" bears little resemblance, attitudinally, to those of the Inland South.

White sandy beaches, hot temperatures, and an endless body of water bring both goods and people from other places and temper their minds as surely as the hills in San Francisco influence San Franciscans.

There is also a commonality between the Gulfers and their southern cousins on the Atlantic. Call it a salt-water connection. Tampa, as an example, is closer in business attitudes to Baltimore than to Chattanooga or to Memphis.

In direct relation to distance from the tide line, the rural agrarian population shows attitudinal ties to the inland rural Southerner. The change is swifter than the upward shift of coastal plain as it pushes north into hills and mountains.

In the Gulf South area, which starts at Fort Myers and wraps its way to Galveston Island, one city stands out. New Orleans is an original, geographically inside the boundaries of the Gulf South, but spiritually unbounded by any classification. It isn't much wonder, then, the business community is staunchly original, too.

New Orleans, a steadfast freehold, has the influence of the Mississippi River laid over a tradition from the Latin Spanish, the semi-Latin French, the unLatin frontier America, an assortment of swamp dwellers, and a liberal spicing of blacks with varying degrees of American Indian and white blood mixtures. Business is conducted in New Orleans in a manner which is unreproducible, at least in this country. There is a sense of time unlike that used by the rest of executive America. Not the mañana of Mexican heritage from farther west, but a deliberate disdain for indecent speed.

Becoming part of the business clique here is a difficult accomplishment because the established hierarchy is precisely that, Established. An aristocratic clubbiness prevails.

Money must be made without abandoning style. The need for action, to be competitive with the world, and a demand for grace come into conflict, making a large part of the business community rather schizophrenic.

New Orleans shares little with her rural neighbors. There are food similarities, but the agrarian people look on New Orleans as a metropolis, with all the sin and corruption present in all metropolitan areas.

Move north to Shreveport and the New Orleans impact vanishes, replaced by influences from Dallas and Houston. Travel west, into Cajun Louisiana, and the city is revered. Cajun Louisiana, at the southern end of the state, is another anomaly—as different from all neighbors as New Orleans is different from other Gulf cities.

Cajun Country is culturally apart from the rest of Louisiana. Or the universe, for that matter. It is the only French-speaking portion of the United States and has French customs more akin to Quebec than Paris. These are modified, however, by life in the swamplands.

The Cajun business community, while having its own ways, is factored by another grand American influencer, the energy seekers. In this case, the assimilation is with the Texas-Oklahoma oil patch. This intense force makes conducting business even more bizarre than the Cajun way of life, the French language, or the Louisiana state law.

Law in Louisiana, by the way, creates some interesting business conflicts because it is based on the Napoleonic Code of justice instead of English Common Law as in the other forty-nine states. Differences are more than casual, as many business executives have learned, especially when dealing with real estate and minerals.

New Orleans and the Cajun portion of southern Louisiana stand apart from, but are included in, because of geographic proximity, Inland South/Gulf South. It's not a good "fit," but these eccentric places don't fit anywhere else either.

INDUSTRIA *(Western New York, Pennsylvania, West Virginia, Ohio, Michigan, parts of Illinois, Kentucky, Minnesota, Wisconsin, Indiana, and Missouri)*

A scoop of territory—from the St. Lawrence River, along the shores of the Great Lakes to Duluth, then south through St. Paul and Minneapolis, following the Mississippi to St. Louis, then northward in a curve encompassing West Virginia— makes up the segment of America in which heavy industry, coal, and steel, along with almost every other industrial-manufacturing process, has forged a common way of life.

Business attitudes here are akin to those in the Inland South. One major force which alters that picture is unionism. Impact of union solidarity in this manufacturing/industrial/mining/foundry zone has been considerable and shows in many subtle ways. This is an especially sensitive point to be watched by those coming from areas with "right-to-work" laws and other nonunion provisions.

Business executives display a degree of natural homogeneity in attitudes because of a striking similarity of occupation interest.

The largest cities have colonies of executives who exhibit strong relationships with New York. This connection is especially noticeable and prevalent at upper management levels where great similarities can be found. Objects may be similar yet not alike. That's a good description for many business people in INDUSTRIA—similar to their New York counterparts, but not totally like them. In some major cities—St. Louis, for instance—the association appears to extend to a love-hate relationship, possibly better described as an envy-rejection relationship, in which the INDUSTRIA executive feels a little outclassed and compensates by adopting more of the Chicago style.

One of the most interesting points is that none of the largest cities, including Detroit, Columbus, Cincinnati, South

Bend, Indianapolis, Cleveland, or Toledo, displays business attitudes too different from each other. The cities here are uniform, at least as far as the business community is concerned.

HEARTLAND AMERICA *(Parts of Missouri, Wisconsin, Illinois, Minnesota, Oklahoma, Arkansas, north Texas, eastern Colorado, Nebraska, North and South Dakota, Kansas, and Iowa)*

The agricultural center of our nation butts against the Inland South, the INDUSTRIA zone, and continues north across Lake Superior into Canada.

On the west, at the far edge of the Great Plains, the first spires of the Rocky Mountains mark the end of this huge region.

As alike as the view, one endless rolling mile to the next, the attitudes of people in business—ranging from agriculture, animal husbandry, and dairy products to insurance and banking—remain consistent.

North to south, the territory is physically diverse. Moving from the glacier-created lakes of Minnesota and Wisconsin into the flatter, dryer central prairie, there are expanses of trees and vast open plains.

Agrarian pursuits change, too. Dairying and dairy products in the north give way to large-scale harvest of a number of grain varieties.

There is a standard HEARTLANDS business look and style. Aside from a few zones of pronounced accents, managers are readily transplantable, even into smaller communities, if sufficient care is given to local traditions of conservatism.

Wheat and cattle, corn and pigs, milk and butter, land prices, cost of equipment maintenance, transportation to market, and other farm-related topics are the conversation of commerce throughout HEARTLAND. This extends into the larger, more urban communities, and should, as these are issues of big, big business. Many executives in this zone do not dress or speak like their counterparts in other areas, but don't be deceived. Large dollars are at stake and these managers are adept at handling them.

The one intruding ingredient came with the discovery of oil. The same intrepid "oil field trash"—as many of those in the industry glory in being called—that caused a rift in Cajun tradition by petroleum prospecting have made their presence felt in HEARTLAND AMERICA, especially in the southern ranges.

Energy seekers brought the first invasion into this agrarian land since the coming of the motorized harvester. Along with rigs and pipelines came language, customs, and skills uncommon to the farm. This action has abated but leaves behind traces of the oil-field cowboy mindset.

HEARTLAND boasts one city, resting on the junction with INDUSTRIA, that is like the rest of the HEARTLAND in many ways, yet totally different. Chicago would stand out due to size alone, but Chicago is more than just big. It has a personality. Blended from unequal parts of INDUSTRIA, HEARTLAND, and its traditional direct ties with the Economic Capital of the Western world, New York City, Chicago's ambiance is greater than the sum of its parts.

Perched along the edge of Lake Michigan, the community sprawls for miles embracing, as any giant urban complex does, neighborhoods of every ethnic base and economic level.

The Chicago business community, again especially in upper echelons, shows a different attitude from those in other American cities. On the whole, more urbane in their dress and manner and more cultured in their demeanor than their HEARTLAND neighbors, Chicago managers still maintain and communicate a down-to-earth feeling typical of the region.

VASTLANDS   *(Western Colorado, north Arizona and New Mexico, Wyoming, Montana, Idaho, Utah, west Texas, and Nevada less Las Vegas)*

Pick the spot where the Rockies break the slowly rising Great Plain in a ragged rip across the continental United States. Go through valleys, following rugged ridges to the western edges of California's Sierra Nevada Mountains and the Cascades of Washington and Oregon. This area, a VASTLANDS, is empty of people and settlements. It reaches north until earth and ice become indistinguishable, encompassing stretches of forest. Southward, the land is arid and drab. This region boasts an endless emptiness. Climate varies from blistering desert to frozen tundra. Ground cover runs the range from sparse weeds existing between bleached, yellowish rocks to mile after mile of green conifer forests.

Oil patch influence on business met its match here, scribing a few marks but failing to establish its customs.

In the VASTLANDS, the largest cities are close in size to other regions' smaller towns. Denver, to a degree, has succeeded in importing and integrating COMMERCIAL CORRIDOR business customs. Even so, the style and feeling of the region tempered the attitude, manners, and dress of new arrivals until they became brittle, and eventually broke.

Denver deserves and requires special handling. The city possesses a rustic sophistication which attaches it to, as well as sets it apart from, its surroundings and neighbors.

Salt Lake City exhibits deep religious-cultural differences which spear into its business community. Caused by what is, in many ways, a combined state religion and an infrastructure of business hierarchy, differences center on effects of the Church of Jesus Christ of the Latter Day Saints in all aspects of Salt Lake City life. The Mormon Church demands faith and organization from its followers. Pressures on Salt Lake business executives are unlike those anywhere else in the U.S.

The antitheses of Salt Lake City are the created tourist centers in Nevada. Business in Las Vegas (spiritually part of another zone) and Reno, plays on big bucks, literally, as money is shoved across hotel desks, bars, and betting tables in apparently unending flow. These anything-goes areas are in striking opposition to the strict air of Salt Lake City. Yet numerous executives work all streets, as is prudent in a zone where streets are rare. (Reno, incidentally, is not a small Las Vegas. The two are different. Reno is a VASTLANDS city with showbiz glitter added. Its basic attitude is VAST-LANDS. Take showbiz glitter from Las Vegas and the desert would cover the streets. There would be nothing left.)

Denver, executor of mountain business and center for minerals exploration and production; Las Vegas and Reno, centers for people exploitation; and Salt Lake City, center for religious heterodoxy: somehow, it's fitting that the major cities of the VASTLANDS should be as varied and diverse as its terrain and plant life.

Throughout the VASTLANDS, the business community is small. The federal government, to conduct and oversee federal lands and projects, adds to the total number of administrators, but still, there are not many when compared to other zones.

Oil patchers meet timber cruisers and logging camp engineers; miners befriend ranchers; and the usual assortment of attorneys, accountants, bankers, insurance agents, shippers, brokers, and real estate agents meld into one, forming a business community unlike that of other zones, yet owing much to their traditions. It's not a large group, which adds the distinction of exclusivity.

NATURELAND   *(Washington, Oregon,*
and part of California)

Leave out Los Angeles. That's WONDERLAND. And leave out the northern Mexican border. More on that later.

From the Juan de Fuca Straits due south along the geo-
logical fault-ridden strip of Pacific Coast, separated from the
rest of America by jagged mountains, all the way to Baja
California, there exists a kingdom of unified thought and values.

The business community is so involved, financially and
emotionally, in this attitude that is almost a philosophy, as
to turn completely away from norms common to the balance
of America. NATURELANDers have established their own
values for dress, their own codes of behavior, and their own
manners. Their opinions of those who dwell and work outside NATURELAND, and especially, to use their word,
"plastic" executives in WONDERLAND, are kindly. Pity-
ing, yet kindly. It is easier not to think of outsiders at all,
rather than think unkindly of them. It is easy to be magnan-
imous, when serenely possessed by faith in the rightness of
your beliefs.

The cities of NATURELAND reflect the different outlook of its business communities. Outside Seattle and San
Francisco, there are no ultra-highrise buildings. Only what
in many places would be a few central business district me-
dium-risers. Instead, there is excellent provision for green
spaces and park places. The overall effect, when compared
to the balance of the country, is urban underdevelopment.

Tacoma, Portland, Spokane, Seattle—all these cities have
a turn-of-the-century, Jack London, off-to-Alaska feeling, which
might be expected, since the entire population of NATURE-
LAND seems to live there in order to feel closer to forests,
ferns, and water. In reversal of outside world tradition, the
sense is that executives in larger cities would like to trade
places with managers in smaller environs to be yet closer to
the land. The work ethic is different, too. Executives are
keenly aware they are selling a part of their lives. They do it
to earn enough to stay in God's Country.

Throughout NATURELAND, there is a sparcity of people. Overcrowding hasn't occurred in most cities yet. By the

time it does, those living there intend to have taken care of all conservation issues, thus preventing the usual difficulties with water and land pollution.

Much has been written about the mild climate in this region. It is mild. And in the north, wet, too. This only seems to make those who reside there hold more intensely to an attitude which demands: "Love it or leave." Those who stay love it and have no intention of leaving.

Seattle, a town with eight buildings 500 feet tall or higher, boasts what may be the only organization of business managers and community boosters in the nation whose goal is to denigrate their city. An unofficial, somewhat tongue-in-cheek group, semi-organized by a newspaper writer, has the avowed purpose of giving outsiders the impression only maniacs would live there. Members have been asked, for instance, to add a paragraph to letters, or a moment's conversation when talking long distance, about how miserable the weather has been, is, and is expected to be.

Large companies headquarter in Seattle. They operate immense, international hotel chains, engage in banking, and manufacture in metal. Those corporate offices are there because management and executives like it that way. Sure, ample hydroelectric power is sold at favorable rates, and a good work force is available. That's reason enough to locate a manufacturing facility. But a headquarters? Corporate offices go where CEOs want them. Some want to be in NATURELAND. It's compromise enough to have to live in a city.

San Francisco is another matter. Quality of life is still a concern because the place is part of NATURELAND in spirit. Its differences, however, are highly visible.

San Francisco has the tallest buildings in the zone: fifteen of 500 or more feet, most in odd shapes. There seems to be something in the soul of NATURELAND executives that abhors a simple square or rectangle. In San Francisco, the pyramid is supreme. San Francisco is different. Period. Even from the other population centers on the Bay noted for a laid-back, kicked-out, anything-goes-as-long-as-it-doesn't-harm-the-environment-or-change-life-quality.

Business executives sense this, as it creates a pecking order. Palo Alto or Santa Clara success is fine, but San Francisco achievement is notably better.

Across the water, in the Oakland-Richmond population corridor, much of the NATURELAND ethos is diminished. It is reboosted in Berkeley, and to a lesser degree, in El Cerrito, and assisted by the ever visible mountainous foothills. But Oakland itself, as far as the business community is concerned, is NATURELAND's free trade zone. Accordingly, it has miles of docks, warehouses, and unsightly commercial space.

The southern region of NATURELAND is based in San Diego. In between San Diego, site of two conflicting cultural attitudes, and San Francisco, which is, beyond doubt, the freest city in the Continental U.S., there is a dropout—WONDERLAND.

WONDERLAND   (Small slices of California and Nevada)

Los Angeles defies description. Sociologists and cultural geographers tell us most fads that sweep the U.S. begin here. Those that attain national acclaim are the best of the lot. Imagine those that don't. In addition to fad generation, Los Angeles, as an area, influences American thought, partially because of the motion picture.

There is an even larger expanse of land where the Los Angeles credo, which credits the natural life but in a jazzier fashion, rules. Geographically, it extends east through Palm Springs to Vegas and south past Laguna Beach. It is such a weird aggregation as to be deserving of a name to itself. Nothing fits better than WONDERLAND. A person with Alice's savoir faire is right at home. The operating concept is: "Don't ask. If you feel it, do it."

In WONDERLAND, managers "do lunch" and pay by

"doing check." They are either uptight in a mild, southern California way, on the hunt for success, or laid back into a subset which may be termed "surf Nazis." The act of showing one's self to be better than one's peers is widely practiced and knows few bounds. Symbolism is the route. Pricey symbols, which cause observers to blanch at the conspicuous cost, set one apart from and above mere mortals.

This outlook is prevalent in the business community, which is also an anomalous aggregation of free spirits. Bankers dress and act like movie producers, movie producers like New York cab drivers with gold chains. There is a hard core of conservatives who see themselves as conservatives. In Richmond, Virginia, they would be ostracized radicals.

Another active force at work in WONDERLAND is encountered for the first time in segmenting America. The Latin influence has a great impact on Los Angeles, but little on its business community.

MEXICA (Central and south Texas; southern New Mexico, Arizona, and California)

Traditional Spanish culture, brought by the Conquistadors, acquired a French touch at the hands of Maximilian, as it intermingled with Mesoamerican Indian stock until it was shocked into a New World form.

The present Mexican culture that evolved is as different from that of frontier America as it is from the attitudes of English nobility. The Mexican thought process accepts fate and expects sorrow. Sorrow is the natural, preordained way of life and there is no reason to contest it.

Frontier America's very existence was grounded on the certainty that through hard work, fate can be reshaped by the worker. The purpose of reshaping faith is personal gain. So to gain, an individual must build or reshape his or her environment.

These two conflicting views have met and clashed over a century in a long strip of southwestern United States. MEXICA is this battleground. Most of its territory was at one time claimed by Spain, and later Mexico.

San Diego, in the west, is the terminus city. Houston anchors the eastern border. Like San Diego, Houston also plays a dual role, bridging two cultures. In the case of Houston, though, it is hard to judge if the influences of the Inland South or the Gulf South dominate. To a great degree, it's an equal pressure situation.

All this has a profound effect on its business community. As has the fact that, in 1958, Houston was at best a one-horse town with pretensions. It has grown a great deal since but maintained its pretensions. Growth brought hordes of new types of business executives, who have met and melded with the old guard. Latin influence on the city is increasing, especially in the last decade. Latinos in Houston come mostly from Mexico, although there are natives of Cuba and several nations in Central and South America as well.

The Mexican-Anglo conflict of philosophies has been felt again and again. It is impossible to be in business in Houston today without being aware of the confluence of cultural attitudes taking place.

Houston started from whole cloth as a land speculator's dream. In fact, it was the dream of two speculators. There have been opposing business groups in the city since its founding days. Once, they couldn't agree which of two streets would be the main axis of the central business district. So they built imposing structures on both, each claque going its own way.

Oil has dominated the city's economy. And still does. Houston is sufficiently oil oriented as to have become the second home for almost every oil patch executive. Since it is difficult to imagine why anyone would deliberately duplicate the ugly urban sprawl of Los Angeles, it must be assumed

Houston happened, as opposed to being planned. Evidence is seen in the lack of zoning. The last time a zoning option was presented to voters, it was overwhelmingly defeated.

In any case, the business group or groups in Houston are unusual. Executives in smaller communities of the area tend to trust Houstonians and distrust the more sophisticated manners of those from Dallas.

From the barrios of Houston, MEXICA spreads north to Dallas, south along the coastline to the border of Mexico, then due west, holding about that same band width to the Pacific Ocean.

San Antonio, two hundred miles west of Houston, shows the Mexican influence most dramatically. The city's established Anglo community, which dominated politics for decades, accepted a charismatic, enthusiastic, action-minded mayor of Hispanic heritage. This unheard-of event is topped by the inclusion of Latin surnames into all walks of public and business life, bringing new depth to a once staid, overly conservative city.

The business community in Alamo Town has responded to the cultural interchange and Mexican influx. With well over half the population boasting Hispanic heritage, and an avalanche of undocumented aliens arriving from Mexico seeking work for a week, a month, or a lifetime, San Antonio is a bilingual, bicultural predecessor of the MEXICA city of tomorrow. Executives and managers here have a different outlook on America and their roles in business.

The MEXICA zone dips under the rich west Texas edge of VASTLANDS, skirting the centers of Midland and Odessa, where oil patch, in its purest form, defines the business attitude.

Rolling over El Paso, where it is hard to tell from the language spoken which side of the Mexican border is which, MEXICA bumps through the arid Southwest. It slips by the Las Vegas anomaly, passes into and is absorbed by Los Angeles, and rests lightly against the attitudes of NATURE-

LAND. Throughout its sweep, the bicultural influence, as well as conflict, is felt and appreciated. This molds business customs in new ways, creating essential and interesting differences.

The fact of Mexican influence is important. Other cities, including New York and Miami, have absorbed Latins. Mexicans are apart from the Cubans of Miami or the Puerto Ricans in New York. Both these distinctive groups, while sharing some of the same heritage, are the result of different responses to different environments and problems. Neither has so completely integrated the pre-Columbian native Indian influences as well or as thoroughly as Mexico.

After over a century of white dominance, MEXICA is now undergoing a balancing of power at all levels. Surprisingly, this cultural confrontation has not resulted in disruption. There have been pockets of problems, but in large, progress and cooperation. Not to mention integration.

Part of the reason for this collaboration is due to the desire of Mexican-Americans as a whole to remain a distinct entity. Unlike many other ethnic groups, which with time have been fully absorbed into mainstream America, those of Mexican heritage in this zone held to themselves for decades. Regardless of the "whys" behind their action, the result is a vibrancy and community spirit now starting to show as an important factor in the economics of the region.

Needless to say, the business community is responsive to this force and marked by it.

Dallas, the northernmost point of MEXICA today, is just beginning to sense the impact. Dallas is a Saint Louis without the River, a Chicago without the Lake, a smaller COMMERCIAL CORRIDOR city with a Midwestern twang. Influences from MEXICA have begun to color the thinking of the business community and are not yet discernible in manners or behavior. Time will change this. Dallas and, to a lesser extent, Forth Worth, its rural, bucolic neighbor to the west that has remained more "cowtown" than its cosmopolitan sister, are in a state of transition. Transitional states are interesting because they produce a variety of viewpoints, along with a wide selection of attitudes.

Dallas, San Antonio, and Houston are a rare combination because nowhere else in the U.S. are three of the top ten largest cities found in one state, in a triangle less than three hundred miles on a side. This geographic closeness promises, long term, a growing together in spirit as well as body. Influences of MEXICA are working in this direction at a heady rate.

One other city in MEXICA merits individual mention. Phoenix is part of MEXICA geographically, yet has an attitude mixing WONDERLAND and small-town HEARTLAND. With powerful boosterisms in the '60s and '70s, Phoenix had a quick boom and is now locked in a struggle to codify its abnormal growth. Business attitudes still reflect leftover boosterism and are just now coming in contact with MEXICA potential.

Another distinctive American city needs discussion. Miami is more than vice. It is, to many, the financial capital of the Caribbean and Central America. Latin influence, as noted, is predominantly Cuban, which translates to aggressive business with none of the mañana syndrome associated with MEXICA.

Miami, like other interesting, different-from-their-region cities, is as much a state of mind as a place. All comers are welcome at the tables of commerce and there is a relaxed, yet intensely focused, play-your-best-shot deal-making attitude. In many ways, Miami is an entrepreneur's dream. Overlaid, like all dreams of success, with the ominous threat of sudden failure.

These are the divisions of America intended for use in discussing variations in business manners, customs, behavior, and dress.

The classifications will undoubtedly bring forth quibbling protests and immodest disclaimers. So be it. There are always malcontents.

Based on these divisions, which will be referred to in the following chapters by the indicated names, exploration and detailing of differences in behavior of business groups can be catalogued and discussed.

Three questions point the way for the next chapters:

1. What are the differences?
2. How significant are these differences?
3. By area, how are these differences displayed?

CHAPTER

3

SPEECH AND BEHAVIOR STYLES

It's not what you say.
It's what you mean.

"*I didn't say I didn't say it. All I said was, 'I didn't say I said it.'* "

—Ronald Reagan

One member of a vice-president's staff has failed, for the second time, to deliver a needed report prior to an executive staff meeting. The vice-president will have to attend the meeting and hedge, or simply admit to not being prepared. Needless to note, he is irked.

The vice-president knows the staffer is at fault, but also that completion of the report depended upon information promised by others in the organization. The situation has generated considerable tension.

What the vice-president says to the wayward staff member, as well as how and when it is said, is a matter of regional variance.

Regional variations in speech extend into two broad areas. The first is accent. Pronunciation, number of syllables given each word, and vocabulary combine with other elements to give a specific sound to our spoken words.

Differences in pronunciation are widely documented and most business executives have experienced many common variations. The so-called "Southern accent," the "Brooklyn accent," and the "Texan accent" are all ingrained in folklore. Anyone interested in various accents across the United States (some are unique and almost unknown) should refer to any of the studies which combine audio material with the printed word, so descriptions and explanations of sounds can be heard.

The second variance centers on speech patterns. Ending a sentence with a rising inflection; sentence pauses; expression of an emotion through word formation as opposed to word selection; and equal-to-equal, superior-to-inferior, inferior-to-superior tonal varieties are a few of the considerations in this subject.

Several of these features will be touched upon in the chapter dealing with the telephone. But enough others remain to demand separate treatment.

Apart from speech patterns, but associated with them, is another, more difficult to define variation centering on propriety of address. Individuals, especially business executives, in various parts of the nation have broadly different notions of what constitutes proper speech under certain conditions. Personal and emotional pressures also enter into the picture, making generalization even more difficult. Observations, however, are possible. Interestingly enough, there is a close parallel between information collected here and accepted folklore.

Given: the situation as outlined, with errant staff member about to be chastised by the vice-president.

The following rebukes are typical only in the sense of demonstrating the limits of propriety; that is, to show a behavior and language pattern which would generally be accepted in the region as reasonable and proper, under the circumstances.

CONSERVATORY:

"Neither of us will gain over a recounting of your past failings. Suffice it to say that your attention to deadlines has become slack. Improvement is required."

A highly formal rebuke, delivered in private to the individual after the executive staff meeting. The meeting comes first, to better assess the extent of actual damage, then a response in appropriate kind.

The precise, deliberate speech style displays emotion only through the positive intensity of the speaker. Note the absence of any derogatory or personal remarks. It is an impersonal, unimpassioned reprimand, with an implied threat toward future job security.

COMMERCIAL CORRIDOR:

Unlike the CONSERVATORY, where the personal element of damage to the vice-president's career through exposure to the ire of superiors is never mentioned, this becomes the central theme.

"You don't have the report. You don't have the report. This is the second time you don't have the report. There is no reason to ask why you don't have the report. Do you know why there is no reason to ask why you don't have the report? I'll tell you. It's because in five minutes, I've got to be in the executive staff meeting. And if our president asks me any questions and I can't answer them because you didn't have the report, it won't make any difference. He will not care if you did the report or not. Only that I can't tell him what he wants to know."

More personal invective is seen in this style. And a revelation that it is not the report for the sake of the report, or the information which is not available, that is the main concern. It is the inability, if called upon, to deliver a positive, career-improving performance before peers and superiors.

The confrontation is likely to occur in front of others of the same rank as the individual being chastised, on the grounds that the example will encourage the rest not to miss deadlines or let their leader down.

THE SOUTHLANDS:

Open emotion is the norm. And following the CONSERVA-TORY's pattern, no direct reference to how the failure will affect the vice-president's career is permissible. The staffer has let down his entire side.

In another different behavior pattern, the incident will not be allowed to die after one confrontation. There will be at least one additional chastisement, especially if the first is held in front of others. Mention will be made of the failure for days, if not weeks, in unsubtle ways. (The opening words indicate the accent used throughout.)

"Ah don' know whut ta say. (Head shakes slowly.) Let me be certain I understood you, because surely I misunderstood. I thought, for a moment there, you were telling me you did not have the report."

(There is a pause here. The guilty party is compelled by the vice-president to admit guilt and thus participate in the rebuke.)

"So. My first understanding was, regrettably, correct. I am sure you realize the effect your inability to perform has on your fellow workers. They did their jobs. Each as demanding as yours. Some more so. They did their jobs, even if they had to come early and stay late. You have not done yours. It is shameful, and you should be ashamed, to have let down and dishonored your friends and associates in this manner." (It goes on. And on. In the SOUTHLANDS, brevity in such matters is unknown.)

No SOUTHLANDS rebuke is complete without invoking honor. A failure of honor is the ultimate failure. And every failure may be flexed into a matter or question of honor.

INDUSTRIA:

Explosions of temper almost never happen face-to-face. Some occur on the telephone, as will be seen in another chapter, but seldom face-to-face.

Reprimands are delivered in private: man-to-man, or woman-to-woman, or man-to-woman, or woman-to-man. You get the idea. There may be a little cursing to add punch. (Acceptable for both sexes.)

"Hell, Bob. This is the second damn time you told me you'd make the play, then dropped the ball. What in the hell are you trying to do to us? Make us look like bush leaguers? You know those two other groups are just waiting for things like this to happen, so they can step up to the plate. Now, come on. I don't care what happened or why you didn't get the information. It doesn't matter. What matters is, you didn't get it. From now on, get your head in the game and get it. I don't care what it takes. Just deliver."

The "team" concept is one that gets high usage throughout INDUSTRIA. This leads to many sayings derived from athletics. Since sports-speak is the official jargon of command, women have learned it, too.

There is no reference in any fashion to the impact of the failure on the superior's position. Such a comment would show personal vulnerability, an unthinkable display.

HEARTLAND AMERICA:

Straightforward, down-to-earth. The basic belief here is that each person knows right from wrong, wants to do right, but as humans do, can fail.

"You haven't got the report? Boy! That sure fixes us into a mess. If they ask, I'll have to tell 'em. That's for sure. Not goin' to do either one of us any good. Isn't this the second time you had trouble like this? What's happenin'? Can I help? Not like you to mess up the same deal twice."

With open admission the missing report will hurt both their chances for advancement. No recrimination, no matter how bitter the vice-president feels. The required offer to help the junior executive solve the problem is coupled to limited praise for normally demonstrated work ability.

VASTLANDS:

Man-to-man is the style, and if a woman's involved, confusion ensues. It's impossible to get man-to-man with a woman.

"Jesus Christ, Tom. That's twice! And twice I gotta go in there and look stupid. What's the problem? You got to get this straight or they are gonna tear me a new one. And before mine goes, yours goes. Now stop screwin' around and see what you can get me in the next five minutes."

With a woman, comments might fall into this general style.

"Ah. Don't have the report yet? Ah. Well, I sure do need it for this meetin'. Ah, ah, is there some kinda problem? I hate to mention it, but this is the second time. Tell ya what. Get me what you can right now, and we'll talk after the meetin' about how I can help you get it next time."

No difficulty in admitting the personal problem caused by looking bad in front of management to another man, but never to a female. Expressed willingness to help the woman, based on the concept the poor little lady can't help herself.

In both cases, not having the report for a second time confuses the manager. People just aren't supposed to behave that way.

NATURELAND:

Team spirit. The crew that pulls together, wins together. If one lets down, all are let down, the leader no more than the rest.

"Couldn't get the report completed, eh? Numbers came too late to work them through the system? That makes it tough for all of us, Paul. Doubly tough for those who had their stuff in on deadline. Look. We've either got to pull together or we'll be pulled apart. We're a crew and we've got a job to do. As a crew, we can do it. If you get behind again, get some help."

The suggestion of getting assistance from other team members must be seen two ways. No self-respecting, individualistic pioneer ever asked for help. Seeing need, others might volunteer, but the intrepid never ask. Instructions to request help badly dent self-image.

The implication the job is too large for the junior, made through the same "get some help" comment, also rankles. In NATURELAND, every man is expected to take big bites, then somehow manage to chew. That's the mark of a real NATURELANDer. And it goes for women, too. Although there are fewer females in executive ranks in this zone, those who have attained such positions are deemed to be possessed of the same pioneering spirit. The identical speech would be used if the culprit were female.

WONDERLAND:

Deleted from the speech are muted cries of "mea culpa, mea culpa" spilling from the lips of the failure. The error, as you can see, is taken personally.

"I'm ruined. Ruined! All my hard work shot to hell because some asshole can't get his (her) shit together long enough to hack out a simple little report. A report a kid could do. But not this guy (gal)! Oh, no. God as my witness, I am patient! The first time, I say we all make mistakes. Now twice? I say, what are you trying to do, assassinate me? Humiliate me in front of the top gun? I'm ruined! And I'll tell you one thing, if I'm flushed, you'll swirl out first. I'll get you promoted, so you can be fired from a better job. I really can't believe you don't have it. I just can't believe it. Tell me you're kidding. You're lying. If I get it over this, you're gonna get it, too. If I . . . ."

Total focus is on damage done to the vice-president. Threats are a matter of natural routine. The question of a possible plot is not rhetorical. Nor is it, in the mind of a WONDERLAND executive, completely out of the question. Such things have happened and, everyone knows, can happen again.

MEXICA:

Machismo forbids much of an exchange because the man causing the problems knows he is in the wrong and might therefore fight physically to assuage his feelings rather than admit he was in any way at fault or incapable of doing the job.

"Don't have it? Did you know the deadline? Isn't this the second time you've missed on this? Please get me what material you can before this meeting."

The tone is vital here. Formal and cold. Impatience hides in every word.

It's brief because there is no way to swear at the recalcitrant. There is also no way the vice-president is going to admit this setback will have any effect on his career. That's the old machismo at work again. Or still. With some, it never stops.

There is no way a woman would get herself into this situation, and if she somehow did, all the VP would have to do is attend the meeting and say some female on his staff had dropped the ball. For the second time. The other attendees, all men, would commiserate with him. The president would understand because what can a man do in the face of such help. A new deadline would be set. If the report were vital, the president would suggest taking the matter from the hands of the female and giving it to a male.

In dealing with a man, there is a good likelihood the individual would be summarily fired from his position. The crime is not the report as much as placing his superior into a position where he looks bad to his boss.

If the man gets fired, he will blame his boss, not himself. Again, self-image is all, and admission of a mistake ruins the image.

WASHINGTON, D.C.:

Nothing much would be said. Who would notice? It's only been missed twice. Enter it into the record later. Unless you have a grudge to settle, why carry on over nothing? If so, then use the failure for all you can.

MIAMI:

Same MEXICA response, but the speech would be delivered with more dramatic zeal: more pain and passion and sadness at being failed by a trusted associate. (Remember, MEXICA society inherited the Mexican tradition, which expects failure and feels the futility of fighting against it. Miami is more of the Cuban-Caribbean-Latin tradition, with hope for success in all undertakings combined with an eager willingness to extract any possible pathos from failure.)

It is, of course, difficult or even impossible to slip into sample scripts the abruptness, the patient exasperation verging on sarcasm, and the fear felt by the victimized vice-president. In real life they are abundantly present.

Also not touched upon is a tactic devastating to the male yet seldom utilized by female executives. Crying.

Tears are responded to regionally on the basis of the degree of sobbing exhibited by the woman. This is not to imply crying while conducting business is common female, or for that matter, male behavior. It is not. But crying does occur in the office. Usually, the originator of the tears is female.

Because of rather strict traditional expectations, it is almost unheard of for a man to cry on the job. Psychologists also note that the female human cries more frequently than the male and generally shows more emotion in various situations. Whether this is due, as some feel, to physical differentiations between the sexes or is a learned behavior, with males learning to be less visibly emotional, is a matter for discussion. Not here, though.

Our task is to see differences that exist regionally when a female sheds tears in an executive confrontation such as the one just reviewed.

Several regions react the same way, but for different reasons. In the CONSERVATORY, tears are so out of place in the office, a crying female will be asked to leave until she can conduct herself properly. There is no way to tell the reaction to a male CONSERVATORY executive who breaks into tears. The idea is simply unthinkable.

In the COMMERCIAL CORRIDOR, INDUSTRIA, and WONDERLAND, tears are met with instant contempt. CORRIDOR executives view them as a sign of weakness that has no place in business. INDUSTRIAlites register shock that someone would so forget him/herself as to show inner emotion; they then become embarrassed for the person, and finally, to hide their guilt at possibly having been the cause of so much distress, grow angry. The WONDERLAND executive sees it as a sympathy play and becomes enraged because another person thinks he or she is sucker enough to fall for old hokum like that.

Southern reaction is instant embarrassment, followed by concern that someone may see the man with the crying woman and either enquire what he has done to her or talk about him behind his back. Businessmen might occasionally cry from anger, but would do so alone.

HEARTLAND response is immediate concern, then sternness. The world is too tough a place for allowing any woman to develop such habits. If she wants to cry, let her stay home. That's where she belongs anyway. All heart, those folks in HEARTLAND. They really are. But not when it comes to female managers and tears.

Few females in the VASTLANDS. Fewer still employed at executive levels in business organizations. Those who are, wouldn't. Cry, that is. It may happen, as anything is possible. But it is so unlikely as not to merit discussion, which says a lot about a regional attitude in this area.

In NATURELAND, while crying is not an acceptable office practice for either sex, an honest display of emotions will result in an honest response. Tears will bring direct questions: "Why are you crying? Are you angry? Hurt? Disgusted with me? With yourself?" Tears signal immediate in-depth psychological probing to discover and discern the true reason for such behavior. From this can come assistance in modification of such behavior. If you don't want help, don't cry, baby. Tears are a psychological plea, and when you're in a society that practices wellness as a religion, you do not wish anything you do to become an attention-attracting exhibition.

Tears in sun-dried MEXICA are wasted water. If that's not crime enough, they are an insult to the macho spirit. Men can cry, under duress, and preserve their macho image. In fact, it is mandatory Macho to cry upon several occasions, none of which is even remotely associated with the conduct of business. Women are known to cry all the time: at home, in the confines of their own surroundings. Who knows why women cry? Who cares? No woman would cry in the office. Tears come from little girls, who should not be taken seriously anyway.

In all regions, tears are not a good idea. Then again, when crying, no one is doing it because it is a good idea. Tears just appear.

A short discussion on accents is in order. In the United States, where many languages are regularly spoken, and English is the accepted national tongue, there is tacit agreement and concurrence on a single, national standard sound. Generally known by some variation of the term "Middle American," this speech is regarded as an accent neutral enough to be understood in any town or city and recognized as cultured speech at virtually every level of American society. The Mid-American sound is the standard for radio announcers and TV news hawks. We hear it every day from the mouths of professionals. But we do not speak it.

Our lingua franca is regionalized. Breakouts of the U.S. used in this book each have a particular sound native to the zone and several subdialects with their own accents.

Many business people in a given area consciously or unconsciously pride themselves on the depth of their accent when speaking in front of those from another place. Others attempt to hide accents, which is an impossible accomplishment without intensive training.

In the past few decades, presidents of the United States have presented us with a wide array of natural U.S. accents. We have had Mid-American, the unique twang and sharp "A" sound of the CONSERVATORY, the clear HEARTLAND, the Texas hill-country accent from MEXICA, the pleasant California smooth speech, and the Southern drawl. These diverse styles come from intelligent, wealthy, successful men. Their wives spoke in similar tones. Why, then, do certain accents still have more "social" or society acceptance than others?

Accent is clearly not an indication of the ability of a person to think, or to have taste, or to have absorbed an education. But a bias remains. It stigmatizes the speaker. Yet accents give our language color and vibrancy. They are regional variations that continue themselves. They are racial indicators that remain long after the last visual trace of race is so mixed and absorbed as not to be discernible.

A prime example of this is seen in the New Orleans phrase, "Relax an' enjoy you'self." Said in an accent more akin to Flatbush or the Bronx in New York than to the magnolia

South, the sound of the words has been unchanged for decades.

Several of the most common accents found in America are listed below. Next to each is the summation of attitudes expressed by business executives. This is a sort of free association in which, given the word listed as the name of the type accent, respondents supplied mental images without considering their validity or contemplating possible insult. Here, differences are shown by the consistency of response, which indicates stereotyping on a national scale.

Accent title	Response
Boston	Uppity. Superior. Cultured. Affected. Shrewd. Conservative.
Brooklyn	Street smart. Lovable but uneducated. Uncultured.
Southern	Unsophisticated. Country. Inexperienced. Cunning.
Philadelphia	A sharpie. Street smart. Quick-witted. Fast with a hustle.
Texas	Country. Uncultured. Uncouth. Loud. Brassy. Braggart.
Spanish	Wily. Emotional. A lover.
Western	Masculine. Rugged. Independent.
Michigan	Bright. Quick. All-American.

That brief sampling gives the idea. The above accents and image responses are intended to show there is a discernible impression attached to each accent, and that when we hear an accent, our minds are biased toward or away from the speaker by our preconceived conception of the type of person who has that accent.

Interestingly, individuals with pronounced accents agree they see the impact of their speech on those from outside their region. And that often, the effect is negative. More, they also say it requires additional effort to disperse bias caused by their pronounced accents.

In business, this can work both ways. At home, the accent identifies the executive as a native, even when dealing with strangers. Away from his or her enclave, the accent will immediately identify the executive or manager as "different" and, human nature being what it is, creates an added obstacle to overcome. Remember that accents are not action. We should be judged by what we do, not by how we sound when we speak.

A final speech difference, based on regional behavior, lies in word choice. Vulgarities, cursing, and uncouth language have, as anyone will attest, little place in business. There is, according to common agreement, no occasion to use vulgar words, swearing, or cursing in business-speak.

If that's the case, why is it done every day and at every level of the executive ladder, from the most junior to the chairperson? Not in periods of emotion, stress, or elation, but in casual conversation? Not by men when alone with other men, but by men and women, in all degrees of segregated or mixed company? Why are there so many scatological phrases to describe the events, processes, and negative consequences of doing business? If the use of vulgarities is not accepted practice, as is commonly felt, why do so many participate so often in the use of these phrases?

The answer is simple. Rude rejoinders, bawdy talk, vulgar sentiments, and all the rest have been a part of language since earliest times. A vital part, as some will argue; an integral part, as all linguists will agree; not an overly imaginative part, judging from the limitation exhibited in originality of expression when calling upon the gods to defame someone or when casting aspersions upon another's ancestry or sexual habits; but important nonetheless.

Among executives in the CONSERVATORY, outside Boston, the mildest swear words (hell or damn) are given new intensity through proper voice modulation and a lingering religious conviction that invoking such potential power can have grave repercussions. Swearing is never done in front of ladies, although it happens, occasionally, in the office because of lapses of self-control. Ladies should never curse or swear. They do, though, especially the under-thirty crowd. It is hard to imagine what the world is coming to.

Boston is another matter. Possibly the intensity of urban life does bring out the beast in humans. It certainly seems to bring out tough language. Swearing during business functions is not without precedent in Boston.

In the COMMERCIAL CORRIDOR, secretaries say stronger words over a broken fingernail than executives do in meetings. Generally, executives are not foulmouthed here. When visiting in other areas, where profanity ornaments conversations, CORRIDOR managers are often surprised.

Considering language heard on the streets of New York City and Philadelphia, it is odd that boardroom phraseology isn't more colorful. A marked tendency to talk business and only business probably accounts for part of the reason.

Among men in the SOUTHLANDS, swear words, curses, oaths, and scatological comments on matters digestive, excretory, and sexual are frequent and often funny. There is reasonable originality here in phrase and content. There is an absolute double standard, too. Men do not use vulgarities around ladies. Ladies, who are not supposed to use them at all, much less know what the words mean, only do so in the company of other ladies. To do so in public would earn them the reputation of being "trash."

The presence of female executives has helped correct this

obstinate moral positioning, but it is still not advisable for women to sprinkle their speech or hear too much when men speak common words. Greater resistance to the use of vulgarities is seen in smaller SOUTHLAND communities, where businessmen segregate themselves more thoroughly from their wives and daughters. And where there are few business-women.

In INDUSTRIA, one of the primary differences between the old, experienced millhand who has risen to mid-management heights and the new, college-trained engineer hired by the firm at that same management level is the liberal use of profanity. The mustang who climbed through the ranks may speak perfectly modulated, precise English, but frequent obscene utterances are a way of life.

The fresh-from-college engineer is more of a quandary. Judging from words heard in otherwise polite conversation by post-adolescents on university campuses, the newly graduated are as entitled to the use of certain words as the up-by-his-bootstraps old-timer. But they are careful not to exercise this privilege. Possibly, control of the tough tongue comes because of their entitlement. The new kid is respectful of the older generation's complete mastery of the more vulgar portions of the King's English. Or, as another possibility, it could be the neophyte, in hopes of advancing, is emulating higher management, who don't swear in public.

In any case, rough language serves as a divider between the two classifications of INDUSTRIA managers and is a reliable guide in determining to which side any given individual belongs. (Age is not always an accurate tool for assessment. Many college-graduated engineers have grown old in middle-management jobs. Even so, they still hold to tradition and are conspicuously careful about their language.)

There is little bias among the younger element against females using the words they hear on a daily basis. Some of the old-timers become a little shocked but secretly seem to like it. They wouldn't want their wives or daughters swearing, mind you, but all in all, if a female is going to hang around the plant, what the hell?

Cursing is a male-only pastime in the HEARTLANDS. And not too much of it at any time, especially blasphemous phrases that take the Lord's name in vain. Women, even when alone, do not use "those words." They undoubtedly think them but would not think of saying them. Rough language is not unknown in business, especially during tense minutes of face-to-face negotiating. But it is not used in the office. What passes between a banker and a stockman leaning against a fence post next to a working cattle pen is between them and no one else.

In the VASTLANDS, language is colorful, to say the least. Everyone uses every word that comes to mind. No restrictions are in place. The more formal the dress for any given occasion, the less swearing and scatology will be heard from either sex. Dressing up is allied to toning down a spicy tongue.

Out here, executives talk like everyone else in every way. Male or female, they select their words for extra impact, when considered appropriate.

In NATURELAND, business swearing is limited, less widespread than in the SOUTHLANDS. It is somehow inappropriate, when standing on a hillside green with giant ferns and the sun making rainbows through the wet air, to use vulgar English. The surroundings are too beautiful and remote to be sullied.

In NATURELAND, foul language in business is heard but not accepted by superiors. If it is heard often enough from the same person, that person will not be accepted. Among peers, there is linguistic freedom. This goes for girl peers and boy peers. Females say what they want, when they want, like everybody else.

In WONDERLAND, most do but some don't. Most do under any circumstance, whenever the feeling strikes. Those who do not, unlike their counterparts in the HEARTLAND, don't grimace or glance disdainfully toward those who do. In business, those who do include both men and women, and they do it together at every opportunity. Whole offices where no one does it exist, but these are infrequent and diminishing.

WONDERLAND produces some wonderful phrases, not to mention intriguingly impossible instructions for having sex with oneself, directions in excretion, and adventurous development of ancestral lines. If you go, do as you like. Everyone else does.

MEXICA is broken into the oil patch, where enormous thought is put into creative cussing, and the rest of the area, where the Mexican language, which contains some colorful phraseology with a charming foreign point of view, slips into everyday English. Men do, women don't. Men do occasionally in offices and at meetings. Women don't. Women do, Southern style, when grouped by themselves. In some cases, when women do, they do it better than men.

At the eastern margins of MEXICA, an old tradition, common to much of the SOUTHLANDS, holds that when a lady repeats any word three times, in rapid succession, she is not cussing. This is useful, and once accepted by fellow managers, an odd condition exists in which, if the female says it three times, no one hears.

Example: Female executive drops a letter. It falls to the floor. She bends to retrieve it, and upon attempting to stand, her head contacts the edge of a desk with a solid "thonk." It is quite painful. "Shit," she says. "Shit, shit." If she speaks the three words in rapid-fire succession, so it sounds like "shitshitshit," or one word, it is permissible.

This custom is not known outside the above-mentioned two areas.

Washington, D.C. is a mixed bag as far as cursing is concerned. It is done, and it's not done. But it's more not done than done because influential individuals from various areas of the U.S., where such talk meets with disapproval in more instances than it is accepted, might be offended. It is easier not to, than to. And safer, too.

Miami street English is as rough as that in any Los Angeles barrio or deep Harlem in New York City. And then a little. Words used are much the same, but there is a Latin persistence on sexual proclivities as a function of familial interpersonal relationships. They can be imaginative. Street talk is frowned upon in the boardroom. It must be remembered, too, that, as in MEXICA, Spanish is the root language. If we are to believe no less an expert than Ernest Hemingway, talk of sexual acts is common tongue for both men and women. These phrases lend flair to drab lines and naturally find their way into polite, as well as impolite, conversation.

Thus far, we have considered profanity only in the context of normal conversational language or as an antidote to pain. There is, of course, another typical time for use of strong words.

When angry, individuals, executives included, speak without recourse to calm reason. Voices rise and words are uttered in an effort to hurt or defend or defy.

In business, anger is often used, especially in the COMMERCIAL CORRIDOR and WONDERLAND, as an intimidation tactic. An executive shows anger to demonstrate or claim superiority over another.

Then there are those who are simply too unruly to contain their tempers and allow themselves to vent spleen in what are actually childish tantrums.

All who fall into either category—and despite our best intentions, most of us do at one time or another—are strongly advised to avoid cursing or name calling. In MEXICA, fist fights are not an unknown result of such anger-inspired carelessness, and more than one murder has occurred as a result of such foolishness. Similar but less stringent physical reactions have also been recorded in the VASTLANDS. Less severe but still dangerous responses are seen in the SOUTHLANDS.

A good rule, anywhere, is to watch your mouth and choose your words with caution when aroused. Hard to do, perhaps, but less taxing on the body if action takes a corporeal turn. Besides, this kind of anger, much less angry words, has no place in business.

In closing the subject of speech variations, it seems only fair to note that we are as we speak. Our accents, our use, disuse, or abuse of certain impolite words, our speech patterns, and other speech-related characteristics come together in each voice to express a facet of our individual personalities. By hearing one another, we form opinions of our business colleagues. But by voice and words alone, we cannot make judgments.

CHAPTER

4

ELEVATOR
ETIQUETTE

*First on or off depends on
who and where you are.*

One pleasure executives have in common is elevator riding. Executives must find elevator riding pleasant, as they do so much of it. There are no published statistics, but if a person has offices on the thirtieth floor of a building, he or she will easily travel up and down more than two miles each week and spend almost sixteen minutes cooped up with strangers.

The elevator is a unique public gathering place. When doors glide silently closed, passengers are in an isolated environment, being lifted or lowered by automatically controlled mechanisms beyond their ken, but not beyond potential failure.

Certain types of jokes on elevators exceed mere bad taste. They are alarming. One otherwise shy manager, not given to any sort of public display, always says aloud, just as the doors shut, "Let 'er fall." Judging from expressions of fellow passengers, the word "fall" is tasteless. "Rip," as in "Let 'er rip," (a Western apothegm) might be better, but no comment at all dealing with the motion of the machine is appreciated and appropriate. This is true in all regions of the U.S. and probably Europe as well.

There is a definite etiquette and behavior for elevators, and it varies from place to place across America. This force seems to control button pushing, discussing business with associates, and finally, who gets on or off first.

Using our divisions of the U.S., let's consider these points.

The advent of computers has called attention to the ordering of information to fit the needs of a desired project or job. The process of dealing with the first piece of paper which arrives on your desk each day, then going to the next and the next, can be likened to a computer operating in a FIFO, first-in/first-out mode. Likewise, dealing first with the latest piece of information entered, LIFO, for last-in/first-out, can also be useful.

Elevator processing logic, assuming all on board are bound for the same floor, can be called FILO. First-in/last-out. Under this system, an individual would enter, walk to the rear of the car, and wait until it is time to disembark.

Such procedure is orderly but unfair, in the sense that the person who came first and spent the longest time on board, and probably got squashed more than anyone else, has to be last in line. It seems almost un-American, as Americans nationwide hate to be last, no matter what. This is especially true of business executives, who are expected to be first in all endeavors.

So the elementary logic of FILO fails on a test of fairness. It also does poorly because it is far too simple a model for such a complex situation.

Nonetheless, most of the country has acquiesced to the inadequacies of FILO. All but the stalwarts of the COMMERCIAL CORRIDOR, who have developed a counter technique. On boarding, they cluster at the front, forcing latecomers to edge past into space in the rear. This allows for FIFO action. In theory.

In practice, FIFO fails because of Otis's First Axiom of Elevatoring; to wit: no passenger ever goes to a floor desired by another passenger. A corollary holds that the first passenger to disembark will be the furthest from the door, so as to create maximum disruption on departure. A second corollary, stating that the later you are for your appointment, the more riders will select floors lower than yours, readily intensifies the quandary.

Entering and exiting are matters of regional custom if one of two criteria is present:

A. Female passengers (one or more),

B. Your boss, your boss's boss, the big boss, or all three.

Let's begin with rank. Based on positional seniority, the most senior executive does the following:

In the CONSERVATORY, COMMERCIAL CORRIDOR, New York City, Boston, Philadelphia, and Dallas: Gets on first, without regard to others, continues to talk if he or she feels so directed, and makes no effort to lock the door open through use of the "open door" button or by holding back the pressure-sensitive bumper.

In San Francisco and the rest of America, except for WONDERLAND, MEXICA, and NATURELAND: Gets on, holds the door button for all associates, and does not speak until it is clear who is riding in the car. If an upper echelon executive feels the atmosphere is safe, conversation will start while in motion.

In NATURELAND, including Seattle: It's every person for himself, with no respect for rank, and silence. No one on board trusts the enclosed, mechanical contrivance and would rather be climbing a hill somewhere in the forest or possibly using the building staircase, for exercise. All quietly stay alert in case of problems.

In WONDERLAND and MEXICA: Second in command boards, holds the "open door" button, is immediately followed by the third highest, who holds the bumper strip in the door, thus assuring a double lock while the big boss steps aboard.

A *National Custom* (almost) is the moment of silence. With some, it may be the girding before battle—anticipation of danger to come. Others may feel anxious about entering a windowless room, being sealed away from the outside world. Still more appear to be shy around strangers. And they know in a minute or so, they will be in close proximity to utter unknowns.

The reason is moot. But the reaction is mute.

In every region, except one, executives, even those talking animatedly as they approach the elevator, fall silent in the interval between punching the button and the arrival of the car.

This moment of silence is punctuated with furtive glances at those who will share the ride and, once on board, is broken only by great effort as someone asks for a floor because he or she is crammed too far from the control panel to select it personally.

Strangers' arms stretch across faces of other strangers, pressing buttons out of reach. Except in the SOUTH-LANDS, not an "Excuse me" or "Please pardon" escapes a mouth.

Only departure from the car reanimates some. Even then, voice tone and volume indicate nervousness or reticent recovery from the silent period.

The one exception to this nationwide custom? Washington, D.C.

Not coincidentally, Washington, D.C., as will be shown, is also the one area where talking on any subject in an elevator is done without thought or caution. For the place which gave us the famous slogan, "Loose lips sink ships," and a town known for its rumormongers, eavesdroppers, and listeners-ins, Washington, D.C. has the most openmouthed policy extant.

Conversation flows unrestrained between two, or three, or even four government managers, beginning when they congregate. It continues through the silence observed in all other regions while waiting for the car, then presses on re-gardless during the ride up or down.

More, there may be two, even three groups, all talking animatedly, as if each were alone and isolated.

This is probably caused by what seems to be the passion of every executive in Washington, D.C.—being heard by others. That there are so many people saying so much, no one is left to listen is a concept which receives little consid-eration. There is always someone left, listening. Don't let it be you. Valuable time is wasted lingering in silence because if you're not speaking, someone else is.

In Washington, silence may be golden, but talk is money green. Expressed another way, appropriations go whither rhetoric flows.

The second circumstance that generates great variation in elevator etiquette stems from the "Ladies First" rule.

Situation: You are on an elevator with several male and female managers. The car stops at the ground floor. To disembark in a mannerly fashion, what do you do?

In Washington, D.C., the CONSERVATORY, COM-MERCIAL CORRIDOR (especially New York City), and INDUSTRIA: Head for daylight at the first crack of the door. This is doubly true if you are toward the front of the car because those in the rear are coming through. Seasoned elevator riders can attain full speed in two strides, so it behooves one to move smartly. Take no no-tice of the female prerogative, "Ladies First." It is an old wives' tale which will cause you woe if exercised.

Be cautious in smaller communities since local excep-tions exist. When one of the females aboard is a friend of a male rider's wife, that man is liable to behave oddly and go with "Ladies First." In her case only. As soon as she is off, he drives in behind her, showing his actual attitude toward matters chivalrous. Fortunately, there are few elevators in small towns, so this caveat ought not be of primary concern.

Throughout the SOUTHLANDS and HEARTLAND: A gentleman lets the lady exit first. Even if there are two ladies. Or three. Or if the females are not ladies at all— a status difficult to define through observation alone over a period of three or four floors. Females are required by custom almost as strong as law to precede males, as doe deer go first into the open meadow.

Men should never ogle or make "goo-goo eyes" (an archaic expression still used in the SOUTHLANDS) at a female passenger. This rule holds whether the car is in motion or not. For that matter, it is indelicate at best for a male to ogle a fellow male passenger. While unorthodox, it is acceptable for female passengers to ogle male riders. This must, of course, be done in good taste and with discretion. Female riders should follow the indication above, intended for males, and avoid such behavior toward other females in the car. The motion rule applies here, too. It is in bad taste, whether the car is in motion or at rest. We digress.

In NATURELAND, VASTLANDS: Here, a frontier respect for womanhood is felt and expressed. No matter that this respect initially stemmed not from chivalry but from a scarcity of females on the frontier. The rule is still "Ladies First." Unless the lady objects. It may then be necessary to be firm and put her off the elevator first. By physical force, if need be. The rule is "Ladies First," and it will be observed because in NATURELAND and VASTLANDS, males show respect to ladies.

In WONDERLAND: Who knows? As in San Francisco, it is sometimes hard to tell ladies from gentlemen. A good rule for both places is "Courtesy before all," or perhaps, as in German, über alles, above all.

The safest course of action is to assume those who look like ladies, are, and those who look like men, are. Few people in WONDERLAND look like gentlemen. Not to say there are none. But they are rarely seen in elevators.

So, be guided by the identity the other person wishes to present to the world. It is polite, and besides, that's what we all do with our friends and associates anyway.

MEXICA: No question here. Senoritas and senoras first. Caballeros and hombres follow.

Of course, there is an alternate rule. A high machismo index, which can be translated as meaning virile male superiority, but has other overtones as well, causes complete disregard for all things female including, at times, even their sexual allure. Only males may possess machismo. Females behave much the same way, but it's called "uppityness." An extremely macho male, faced with an open door, must:

A. Straighten his posture.
B. Assume a disdainful look.
C. Stride from the car with the air of a torero parading in the ring.

This is an automatic response. Do not be critical. It seems to work and, for some reason, attracts females. In all MEXICA locales, the older generation, men over sixty, have not been reeducated by the Feminist Movement. With them, it is always Ladies First. Unless they are riding with their wives. Then the dominant person in the household steps off, unless she has figured him out and holds back so he feels dominance. She can then shame him with a female look that says, "poor little me." He immediately sees the error in his manners and is embarrassed.

Another elevator problem is especially prevalent in New York. Managers in New York City live in elevators, or feel they do. They haul the most amazingly cumbersome, awkward parcels and bundles up and down with stunning regularity. Not to mention riding with their pets. Outside New York, it is rare to see a dog in an elevator. Such a sight would cause comment in Dallas, or Atlanta, or Phoenix. Canines take passage in New York elevators all the time, in office buildings as well as apartment houses.

So, as a stage setting: You are on an elevator in your office building. The door opens, revealing a potential passenger with a considerable collection of packages under his/her arms. He/she enters. The doors close. There are enough people riding so that when the bundle carrier arduously turns to face the front of the car, at least three people are bumped, stabbed, or prodded by the irregular parcels. (Note that no one rides with his/her back to the door. The process is to enter and turn 180 degrees. Everyone rides facing the entrance/exit. This is probably due to a carry-over from cave person days. Or a survival tactic against being mugged.)

Some bumped passengers are vocal.

"Uhooof."

"Uh. Hey! Watch it!" (Usually followed by "buddy" or "sister.")

In business, politeness is, as always, dictated by position. The astute business person looks at the bundle carrier closely in an effort to determine:

A. If he or she is with the same company, with a client organization, or possibly with a competitor.

B. The relative rank of the package holder.

Naturally, if the overburdened person is of higher position, you should immediately step forward with offers of help coupled to protestation of how little bother it is to you. Common sense dictates this action even if the holder is with a rival firm. One never knows when a kindness will be recalled, especially when seeking a new job or improved position.

Should the individual rank lower than yourself, a state of *noblesse oblige* exists. If one does not correct the actions of underlings, how then are they to learn? It is obligatory to comment. Harshness, as the exchange will take place in public, must be avoided. Some suggested reprimands include:

"Damn, John. Plan better than this. You're inconveniencing these people."

"Come now, Mary. Must think ahead and not overload your capability for smooth performance."

As can be seen from the examples, remonstration should be subtly associated with the job. This establishes your authority, asserts your right to comment, and at the same time, because of insecurity created by such remarks, drives home the lesson.

It is best, if you do not know the burdened passenger, to remain stony-faced and icy-eyed. Comments are unnecessary and will be wasted on anyone who would invade the confines of an elevator with an overload of baggage.

Should you, on occasion, be required to tote an untoward amount onto an elevator, the following ploy will work in any region of the United States. This action lowers the chance of inadvertently bumping someone, stuns other passengers, and actually dissuades potential riders from coming aboard at stops prior to your destination.

Procedure: Arms full, step onto the elevator. Do not try to hide the unwieldiness of your load. Show it off. Do NOT turn to face the door. Stand straight and face the exact center of the rear of the car. This will place you in the middle of the door space.

Say, in a polite but firm voice, the number of your desired floor. Say it once and only once. Say it with authority. Do not, under any circumstances, turn your head in the slightest to see if someone pushed the appropriate button. Speak, then freeze. Fellow riders will be frozen by the break with custom which comes in not facing front.

Potential passengers will be dissuaded because, upon the opening of the door, your body and baggage are blocking the entrance. The appearance, even if the elevator is half empty, is that it is jammed full. Most will not contest your blockage and resign themselves to another wait.

It requires nerves of steel to face the wrong way and raw courage to stand with your back to the opening when you know there are people facing you, bursting with desire to ride. Only the strongest can use this technique. These will be amply rewarded by the success they attain.

Another regional worry concerns hats. In MEXICA, where traditional headgear is high-crowned and wide-brimmed, members of the male portion of the business community remove hats upon entering enclosed, people-occupied space. The "hats off in the house" rule applies. Some of the oil patch old-timers, though, still keep their heads "undercover" even while dining. For those who haven't done time in the military, "undercover" refers not to clandestine spy activity but wearing a hat. The phrase is derived from "covering" the head.

It is impossible to hold a large, western-style hat in a crowded elevator without having it crushed, bent, or otherwise deformed. This can result in strange gyrations by the hat wearer, as turns and twists are executed to avoid the worst damage. Out of frustration, many now leave their headpieces in place while on the lift, ride to the desired floor, and doff it upon stepping free of the car.

Headwear in other parts of the country is more adaptable. While the western style is prevalent in the VASTLANDS and NATURELAND, several types of caps, designed to cover the ears during colder weather, are seen. These present no problem in being held in one's hand, no matter how packed the elevator becomes.

In the SOUTHLANDS, hat wearing among business executives is, according to statistics, on the decline. Among those still indulging, "off in the elevator" is a rule inviolate. No exceptions.

New York City has many styles of headgear. Sweat bands, for instance, always stay in place. Technically, these are head *wraps*, not head *covers*. Even moist from perspiration, they should not be doffed. Or perhaps, one should say, especially when moist.

The foldable hat or cap, as discussed, presents no problem. It should be removed promptly upon entering.

The crown and brim model can present the same difficulties as the cowboy ten-gallon. But off in the elevator it must come. No excuses or exceptions.

Thus far, hat etiquette has been presented basically for men. This is because there is no regional variation in ladies' toppers. Ladies' hats stay on. In parts of NATURELAND and all WONDERLAND, this is one reliable way to tell a lady from look-alikes. Ladies' hats stay on. All styles of ladies' hats. No exceptions.

Briefcases make an interesting elevator problem for business people.

Briefcases, handled carelessly, are vicious knee, groin, and shin bangers, depending upon the relative heights of banger and bangee.

In all areas, good manners and custom dictate that upon boarding an elevator, each briefcase wielder—in many instances that will be everyone in the car—should: s-l-o-w-l-y bring the briefcase from its carrying position at the side to a position across the body at chest level. Holding it comfortably and securely, keep it in front, where it may be used to gently ward off those intruding into your space. In any case, it will be safer in this position.

For proper button-pushing styles, we need to study several regions, as the request from a total stranger to perform a personal service meets with different acceptance in certain areas. Integrated with this is the New York City policy of silence in public, when alone, derived from the concept that if you don't speak to strangers, strangers will not speak to you. While not altogether a reliable social rule, it seems to work as well as anything in New York.

In HEARTLAND AMERICA, asking someone to button your floor is no problem at all. People, even in Chicago, speak to each other in elevators all the time. Most verbal transactions are limited to "Hello" or "How are you?" or "Hot" or "Cold," but there is speech.

In the SOUTHLANDS, a pleasant "How you?" is common. You can ask someone nearer the button board to select your floor, and it will be done gladly. Just say, "Please."

In the VASTLANDS, speech with another person is so highly valued it is not used casually. This results in the need to be taciturn as opposed to garrulous. Asking is no problem as long as it's done civilly. And briefly. "Four, please," is sufficient. Do not gild the lily.

In WONDERLAND, it is best to play by New York rules, which follow. Probably no harm will come from speaking with strangers. It's just that they can be so damn strange. There are fewer people in WONDERLAND than New York, but a greater percentage of those there are, at best, odd.

In MEXICA, ladies will have no trouble having other ladies select their floors. Gentlemen will do so with a flourish and probably a gleam in the eye.

For men, asking ladies is a little different. There is a feeling of taboo concerning conversation between unintroduced males and females. Best advice is to ask once. If she does not respond, it's not because she didn't hear. It's because she doesn't feel it proper. Further conversation on your part will be ineffective, not to say indelicate.

A solution, after one try, is to reach as best you can and make your selection. As an alternative, if there is a man standing closer to the controls, ask him. He will respond.

This brings us to one male asking another male. The request must be made in such a manner as to show clearly the asker does not consider the asked a servant and does consider the act a favor. Egos in MEXICA are touchy on the master-servant angle.

"Excuse, me, sir? Would you please do me the favor of pressing ten, as I cannot reach it without disturbing others?" seems like a long line of talk, but it will salve feelings. Notice, too, the use of a question. Almost all requests from one equal to another are couched in the form of questions.

The INDUSTRIA zone has no problem, if you are direct. An elevator is a mechanical device intended to haul managers up and down. No nonsense. "Six" as a floor request won't get you looked at. "Six, please" will be respected by some for its politeness, but will probably generate a few glances.

In the CONSERVATORY, keep it brief. Your presence on the same elevator, especially in Boston, is a tolerated intrusion to every other rider, as each longs to live a life of absolute exclusivity, apart from others who may not be of the proper class. This is doubly true in Boston, where the rule "Speak, but do not be spoken to" holds. The best technique is to use a slightly bored voice. Don't try for a Back Bay accent unless you've spent time there. Those who know can tell. And all the CONSERVATORY, especially Boston, abhors an imposter.

The COMMERCIAL CORRIDOR presents a difficult challenge. To be safe, apply New York rules to this matter, even in Philadelphia.

New York rules:

1. Safest action: If you cannot get to the button, keep your mouth shut, eyes front, and do not speak even if spoken to. Ride until enough people get off, then press your button. There may still be time to reach your floor. If not, wait until the elevator has traveled to its stopping point, then punch your button and ride.

2. Alternate action for those with experience and confidence. Gaze intently at the person nearest the console, make eye contact to assure attention, then brazen it out. Speak the floor number only, coldly, without emotion. Do not be tricked. Watch until the person has complied with your demand.

3. Action for natives only. Go for it. Stage a scene by pushing your way to the control panel and select your floor. Make your action a clear demonstration that no one but you is in control of your life.

On the subject of disembarking from a crowded car when you have been forced to a position in the rear, only one problem in regional variation exhibits itself. In the COMMERCIAL CORRIDOR, again with emphasis (as is the case for most things) on New York, there appears to be an aversion, stronger here than elsewhere, to touching or being touched by strangers. In parts of San Francisco, body bumping, especially by members of the same sex, might be taken as an invitation. In New York it is abhorrent. Overcome this feeling. Steel yourself for contact. After all, elevatoring is a tough sport. The best defense is said to be a good offense. In this case, while trying not to be overly offensive, refuse to give ground. Do not move to the rear, thus avoiding the problem of back-of-car exits entirely. Once aboard, station yourself at the front, on the side opposite the controls, and hold your ground. Force others to go around you. Say nothing, remain stony-faced, and stonewall the opposition.

If by some chance you are bullied aside and forced to the rear, remain calm. Hold your peace until you arrive at your destination, then explode from the back, forcing your way between those blocking your path. Do not be timid. The elevator door waits for no one. Some also find the use of a sharp karate-type yell an advantage. It serves to gather strength and demoralizes the opposition. In any case, your hands touching others' shoulders and arms as you pry them aside work like electric cattle prods. Those you touch will move—fast.

Across America, the elevator operator is a vanishing breed. Male or female, these dedicated souls have braved the ups and downs of their jobs, exposing themselves to restless mobs and increased opportunity for being infected by a contagious disease through contact with a vast variety of humanity.

Some office buildings, mainly in the SOUTHLANDS and New York City, still have elevator operators. Their once proud task is now lessened because, in most cases, the only control is a button.

When running into operators today, a glance will tell if they are pilots of the pre-1960s hand-control cars or simply fingers pushing buttons. Any under the age of forty are automatically button mashers as opposed to handle rockers. Over forty, it's a judgment call.

Even rarer today than the elevator operator is the elevator starter. This worthy had the task of scheduling the departure of cars and holding them, doors open and clients aboard, until it was clear there were no further passengers. Then, with a dismissing flick of the wrist, the operator was given control of the vehicle to make the run. A good starter would preserve privileges of rank. If a manager of sufficiently exalted position arrived, a car might be held and dispatched just for that executive. Private passage was not a perk given to everyone. It demonstrated status, as well as leaving the impression that the particular manager's time was of utmost importance.

The final aspect of elevator etiquette concerns a habit found in cities with very tall buildings. In these, there are several elevator banks used to give faster service by stopping only at certain floors. The building also has an elevator transfer lobby midway to the top. To reach the highest floors, one rides an express to this lobby, then changes cars to go higher still. It is an analytical problem in motion science to determine the fastest route from the ground to a desired floor. Aiming at the forty-eighth floor, for instance, is it quicker to take the express directly to fifty, then catch a car to drop two floors down? Or simply board the direct lift to the forty-eighth floor and risk making a number of stops en route?

New Yorkers seem to worry about this at length, and a surprising number show considerable ability in mathematics as they toil to derive the quickest method to reach a desired destination.

Chicagoans do not seem as concerned. Neither do San Franciscans. Such mental gyrations are out of character in NATURELAND, but a few still practice the act in Seattle and San Francisco. WONDERLAND has no truck whatever with this line of reasoning, as it is a clear waste of energy to calculate anything.

And so it goes.

Nationwide, there are noticeable variations in elevator etiquette among business executives. New York is the capital of elevator usage and therefore the leader in divergent behavior. Guidelines included here allow insight into the problem and understanding of not just the correct action, but the reason behind the correct action. Remember, when conducting business or traveling from one zone to another, think like those who live there. It will pay big dividends. Best of riding to you.

CHAPTER

5

PARKING LOT PROTOCOL

*Regional use and abuse of the
business automobile in America.*

The advertising team for a major Detroit automobile manufacturer helped create a TV spot in which the central theme
was "America's love affair with the automobile." If ever a
true love-hate relationship existed, it is between the average
American and the car.

One of the largest regional differences in business behavior centers on the automobile. If you work in WONDER-
LAND, you must have one. If you live in Manhattan, having
one is a problem.

Differences go deeper than this because the car, or truck—
popular in NATURELAND, the VASTLANDS, SOUTH-
LANDS, MEXICA, and HEARTLAND—is used in business. The type and make of car indicates prestige, as does a
car furnished by the corporation and the location of your assigned slot in the company parking lot.

Car or truck, male or female executive, the list of auto-
related business functions is enormous.

To study the four-wheel phenomenon, it's best to start
with a cross-country rundown on the relative importance of

the automobile in daily business life and then relate this to specific models and styles of vehicles.

THE CONSERVATORY:

A car or truck for personal and business use is mandatory. Especially in the winter when the snow is so deep, walking or riding a horse, in addition to being cold, isn't awfully practical.

In the CONSERVATORY, everyone seems to live just outside of somewhere. Even if one lived inside somewhere, the towns are of a size to make possessing a car mandatory.

Cars and egos are related here, but in a curious fashion. As opposed to egos demanding satisfaction by possession of the latest four-wheel drive, turbo-flushed, rocket-powered road sled, equipped with assisted automatic everything and price tag to match, there is reverse entropy.

The ideal CONSERVATORY business executive's car is a sensible vehicle, preferably ten years old in perfect condition. This shows the owner is a sober sort, properly frugal. More, it is a clear statement to the world: "I know how to care for my possessions."

In this unusual fashion, the owner's ego is satisfied, there is a warm feeling from a display of practicality, and one's position in the community is strengthened.

This same ego matrix applies in Boston, but it is better to have a ten-year-old Rolls or Mercedes than a Buick or Chevrolet. It makes practical sense, too, because a ten-year-old Mercedes will naturally last longer and look better than a Chevy. Considering it costs about five times as much to buy, it should look at least twice as good after a decade.

Auto dealers in the CONSERVATORY have been known to lay aside selected models when new, age them eight or nine years, then offer them for sale at exorbitant prices. This is a rather unscrupulous way to own and drive a vehicle that is "right." If you contemplate buying such a car, consider the shame if you are caught out by some knowledgeable business cohort who knows your game. You might never live down the humiliation.

THE COMMERCIAL CORRIDOR:

Top executives living in suburban retreats have more than one vehicle. Among those seeking the rustic, outdoor image but with no desire to move to NATURELAND, the truck, in one of its many guises, is better than a station wagon. Some form of transport for a large number of persons is mandatory because of car pools (traditionally driven by the lady of the house) and occasional weekend guests.

The family also needs an inexpensive runabout. This is a car which may be left at the train station all day, used by teenaged kids during the week, or taken for a quick trip to the store.

Finally, there must be a prestige car—Cadillac class or above. Actually, Cadillacs are out. Imports are in. A Mercedes or a Saab, which appeals to the younger executive set, overshadows Cadillac and Lincoln in the Prestige Gran Prix.

Executives residing in urban areas or Manhattan have established another social order of transportation, based not on the make/year of vehicle, but on the availability of a chauffeur. A uniformed driver arriving at the door in any type sedan has more cachet than any self-driven Rolls. Move up to a stretch limo complete with TV, bar, stereo, etc., and the driver-limo combination has more status than a Lear jet.

Among car/truck owners in the COMMERCIAL COR-RIDOR, some of the CONSERVATORY's "pride through age and condition" feeling has rubbed off. A new car is considered great in any price range. Less expensive models need to be replaced each year or two, thus demonstrating the executive's contemporary outlook and fiscal wherewithal. The most expensive units can be held for five or even six years, which illustrates to everyone that quality, up front, is the way to go.

THE SOUTHLANDS:

Throughout the SOUTHLANDS, the pickup or a variation with full body, like a Bronco or Suburban, is as popular as the automobile.

Likewise, the Cadillac, because of its American origin, gives prestige to the executive owner while saying something nice about his or her patriotic attitude. The Mercedes or Jaguar or BMW is respected, but owners of imported, expensive vehicles are deemed tainted by being a little too showy. Remember, this is a conservative area. If you have money and authority, you're expected to let people know it without lording over them or being utterly ostentatious.

Japanese cars carry the same problem when compared to a Chevy, Ford, Buick, Oldsmobile, etc. It's not that most don't feel they are better made and offer more value for the dollar, it's just that there's still a show-off stigma associated with driving the unusual. This is, by the way, a self-feeding phenomenon. The southern business person who buys an import is looking, to some degree, for the opportunity to be different. Fellow executives and associates, who always knew the person was a little odd, now see him/her behind the wheel of an odd car. The cause-and-effect relationship is strengthened.

In general, throughout the SOUTHLANDS, a new car will make up for brand names. That is, a new Chevrolet is better on the prestige scale than a three-year-old Buick, no matter how the older vehicle has been maintained. A new Cadillac scores higher than a new Chevy. But the new Chevy outclasses a five-year-old Cadillac. You get the idea. Swapping a new one for a higher priced model is a trade-off.

The proper southern executive will drive him or herself to work from a suburban home, preferably in a Cadillac or Lincoln. Attorneys, ad makers, and the fashionable accountants, not to mention insurance executives, are allowed their peccadillos. An expensive import is acceptable in this group. The wealthy agro-executive will use a Suburban or other enclosed truck.

Every car, without fail, will be equipped with air conditioning, which will run eight to ten months of the year.

INDUSTRIA:

In this zone, union influence is strongly felt in executive vehicle selection. Having a new car or truck here is like having a Mercedes elsewhere. Management, in an ongoing effort to be one of the gang, plays down car prestige as far as the vehicle driven to and from work. The Mercedes or Volvo or BMW stays home in the garage and is used by the at-home parent. Or the female of the house drives it to work. (A female can do it because everyone knows women know nothing about cars.) Even on weekends, the male executive is careful of being seen in his Euro-barge.

Unionism also impacts import sales in INDUSTRIA. A special irony exists here, in that a cursory examination of employee parking lots reveals countless Japanese-made trucks and cars, in spite of the union-influenced "Buy American" campaign which has run intermittently since the late 1960s. Many workers obviously buy price-value as opposed to country of origin. But the same program has had an impact throughout management, making Buick or Oldsmobile the sedan of choice. Cadillac-Lincoln, reserved for the uppermost echelon, is felt to be a little too demonstrative of position and wealth, so is admired, often kept at home, but seldom seen on the job.

Detroit and environs is no exception to the above general rules, despite the fact that a company-furnished executive car is as common a perk as salary and bonus. Auto executives run their brand through their families. Since they receive use of a new car each year, and can buy last year's at a stupendous discount, they drive them, buy them, and sell them to Uncle Morty and Aunty Lynn or cousin Charles or sister Dagmar.

Prestige in this zone, as cited above, means new. Brand is American. And the overall motive is not to appear too showy.

HEARTLAND AMERICA:

Anything goes in HEARTLAND, as long as it's black, white, or blue, made by General Motors or Ford, with an accepting nod to Chrysler, and is big. "We got lots of distance out here," one sales executive said, "so I need a big car to cover it."

Down-sizing of American cars has not met with enthusiastic reception in HEARTLAND. Replacing the blunder boar of bygone years, various four-door bodies on pickup chassis (which have enough interior space to seat eight, including luggage and other worldly possessions, while still reserving room to serve a buffet lunch) are popular.

Trucks have another advantage. On a farm, with its complex tax structures, a truck can be bought and driven for personal pleasure use, yet still find a place in the deduction column.

Imports are present. Again, smaller Japanese economy units do well and, at the other extreme, the Deutschland duo, BMW and Mercedes, find favor with a certain executive segment that wants a little flash. Not too much, just a little.

To be really in, however, the lesson is clear. Own a truck. A new pickup with a cab large enough to seat four in Spartan luxury is a good investment. Air-conditioned, of course. Even in the northern territory of the HEARTLANDS.

VASTLANDS AND NATURELAND:

The epitome of four-wheel transportation is summed up in these words: "Four-wheel drive."

Having all four wheels apply power to the ground is popular in the CONSERVATORY, the COMMERCIAL CORRIDOR, and through those areas where snow and ice descend for as much as six months a year.

But nowhere has the popularity of this 1980s auto fad taken root and been embraced with such enthusiasm as in the VASTLANDS and NATURELAND. Four-wheel drive signifies the go-anywhere-I-damn-well-please attitude pervasive throughout these areas. In the VASTLANDS, they do go anywhere, by four-wheel drive truck, tearing hell out of the back lands with abandon because there's so much area in which to rip and roar. NATURELAND folks are a little calmer and not so fast to slip into their pristine forests and roar where there are no roads. Their conservation ideology forbids it.

VASTLANDS executive transportation isn't the Mercedes, although there are a few of that manufacturer's upright, slab-sided safari wagons about. The height of prestige is a fully modified truck, sprouting more lights than shine at Yankee Stadium, special snow-and-mud tires, spoilers, bug deflectors, a roll bar, and a yahoo paint job that abandons all pretense to good taste. Any variation of basic truck, including open- and enclosed-bed models, is venerated. To own one is to show your true self.

In effete places like Denver and, to a lesser extent because of social pressure, Salt Lake City, Mercedes maintains cachet, with BMW going to the few who demand performance.

Japanese products fit the same need of those who require value. As would be expected, both LANDS are dumping grounds for smaller Japanese trucks. In fact, never have so few bought so many.

The VASTLANDS and NATURELAND have a simple formula. Four driving wheels equals prestige. If you can't have it, at least doctor your truck to look like it.

WONDERLAND:

WONDERLAND, not Detroit, is the international preserve of car crazies. Car craziness must be contagious, as the majority of the population here seems infected.

Every zany manufacturer, worldwide, who could bum or borrow the money for a ticket to America, arrived in WONDERLAND during the late 1950s and early 1960s and found profit-seeking sharpies to import their peculiar vehicle. Never mind the damn things never worked in their homelands and had a reputation for reliability lower than the mileage indicated on a used car speedometer. It was new and different.

This plethora of auto vagaries sold in WONDERLAND precisely because they were different. Prestige stems from exclusivity. As the auto world settled, the concept stayed. Only the way to be exclusive changed from being nutty enough to buy some hacked together aggregation of pre-World War II spare parts to coming up with the cash for a new Rolls, Mercedes, etc.

The motion picture business brought the concept of weekly payrolls to the area. Hiring by the week became an acceptable way to compensate all but the highest levels of the cinema world. This holdover system opened the door to the idea of leasing. Leasing, aside from its original tax advantages, let the car buff satiate his or her car cravings and still have enough money for groceries and rent.

A Cadillac in WONDERLAND instantly marks the driver and passengers as shameless geriatrics. Unless it is a chauffeured limo. Then they are marked as prosperous patricians.

Import is still the cry, and the Porsche, Dr. Ferdinand's slipstream wonder from Wagner Land, is the ultimate weapon.

Mercedes is okay; BMW fine; Ferrari terrific, but prone to problems only Italians understand or can live with. More exotic than Ferrari? Great. More is better, anytime. But through it all, show up in a Porsche and you know you've arrived.

Company-furnished cars furnish a dilemma for the WONDERLAND executive. All too often, the company is guided by rules established for the balance of the U.S. So they provide a Ford, Chevrolet, or Chrysler for executive use. In WONDERLAND, that's tantamount to establishing a clothing rule in which everyone must appear in conservative, blue, three-button suits. What works outside WONDERLAND fails in the new reality.

Nowhere in America does the automobile have as much power as a statement of the executive's position, prospects, and, of course, ego.

Well, maybe somewhere else.

MEXICA:

Houston is a dividing city between the SOUTHLANDS and MEXICA. Thus, the automotive influences of both regions blend.

Houston is also a freeway city, like Los Angeles, and delivers another level of car taste to citizens.

There may not be quite as much executive ego involved in car selection as seen in WONDERLAND, but if it is less, it's hard to notice. The automobile and the oil patch were made for each other. Oil patch ego is constant and overwhelming. Only material outlets of expression, like the elaborate, expensive car, can relieve pressure.

In the oil patch, company cars are nearly as *de rigueur* as in Detroit. During periods of boom or bust, the number of employees may change, but the perk of the automobile remains. A manager drives a company car. It is almost always a Ford, Chevy, or Chrysler product, although some of

the senior folks get Buicks, and there are even a few Olds-
mobiles cruising about sporting company plates.

At home, however, it's another story. A prestige bomb
sits in the carport, waiting for Daddy. Or Mommy.

If the family is Old Houston or Old Texas establishment,
it's probably a Cadillac or Lincoln. That's what it will be,
too, if that's the way the family wants to appear, but just
doesn't qualify on grounds of wrong blood, too little money,
or enough money but too little time in residence.

For New Houston, the Panzer wagons, from Audi to
Porsche/Mercedes, show money. And because the vehicle is
imported, taste. That's a hard combination to bet against.

Southern influence makes the large four-door, Suburban-
type truck a standard of the executive class. As car-pool com-
muters to the kid's school, transportation to the fanciest stores,
and on the highway to the weekend ranch retreat, this vehicle says "status." From there, down in price, it's the hoi
polloi. The Jaguar has gained cachet, after some have run
long enough to allow the stylish folks to view the lines of the
car with all four wheels on the ground, as opposed to hitched
into the air behind a wrecker.

Throughout the balance of MEXICA, where everyone
drives 65 miles per hour or more, and most stay in the "more"
range, the situation is static.

Wealthy Mexicans can afford and do buy fine automobiles, but seldom drive into the U.S. Too much chance of
custom hassles on their side of the bridge. So they fly in and
rent wheels.

Outside the three or four large cities, the import, except
for a few of the Japanese units, doesn't have much play.
Prestige, in many areas, is having a car that runs. (Everyone
has a car or truck. Many are sitting in a front or side yard
accumulating dust. A running vehicle is a mark of prestige
in itself.)

Trucks abound. South and west of San Antonio, the truck
is the absolute standard means of transportation, as common

as in HEARTLAND. Big trucks are preferred over small trucks, and executives, along with everyone else, drive them as their main means of transportation.

WASHINGTON, D.C.:

Washington, the town, deserves comment because the only vehicle noticed by the executive class is the chauffeured limousine. It's the only one aspired to, as well. If the truth be known, our government is zany about chauffeured automobiles, and no one in management is anyone unless he or she has an assigned car and driver. It's rather an egalitarian perk, because in addition to freeing the manager's mind so he or she can think of matters more important to the people and state, it also employs one of the people. A job is a job, so a car and driver keep one more soul off unemployment rolls, as well as out of the statistics.

MIAMI:

Sun-Sin City shows both its Latin influence and the counter-culture drug money flowing into business by accepting any multi-chromed, fiberglass-bodied creation of demented minds as appropriate business transportation. Limos are in. Even rental autos at the airport come in colors seldom seen in the balance of America.

Cars furnished by the company are perks in many areas of the U.S. These are seldom more than mid-size econoboxes, but since the 1970s, have grown in accessories to include air conditioning and radio.

If, as an executive, you are allowed to use a company vehicle, are there regional do's and don'ts? You bet.

In areas like HEARTLAND, MEXICA, VASTLANDS, or NATURELAND, it is déclassé to allow your spouse or live-in friend to use the company car. You were awarded the car, so you drive it. The converse of this holds true in other areas (parts of the SOUTH, the COMMERCIAL CORRIDOR, and the CONSERVATORY) in which allowing your spouse or live-in to use the vehicle regularly is fine. As long as the IRS doesn't find out.

This change of rule seems to emerge as a function of what is considered, in a given locale, "normal" driving.

Company cars are great perks, but cautious, career-oriented executives must examine the internal workings of their own organizations and industry before accepting such a boon.

If the organization is egalitarian—everyone from chairman of the board on down drives the same make and model car, equipped the same way—then status in the organization cannot be readily derived from the vehicle assigned to a given executive.

Expand that a little. Perhaps the chairman and the president both get luxury sedans; executive VPs, classy midrange units; and the balance of the officers, including assistant VPs, are relegated to white or black economy cars. Status is clearly proclaimed each time the engine is started. In this case, depending upon regional prohibitions, it might be well for the ambitious to leave the econowagon home, either to sit in the garage or be used by the co-resident. This allows managers to turn in a pristine, low mileage car, showing their care for corporate property.

It also permits driving a vehicle in the class next up the career ladder. This improves status. And we all know that how we are perceived makes us what we are.

Driving the next highest level vehicle is not as expensive as it sounds. Since the company will trade units at some preordained mileage, usually under thirty thousand miles, auto wholesalers in your area can be approached to stay alert. It's almost assured one will become available in a short period of time and can be bought for thousands under retail cost of a new model.

In many industries, especially those requiring direct contact between technicians, engineers, or sales personnel and their customers, cars or trucks are used to make rounds. This is common throughout the oil patch, in the VASTLANDS, INDUSTRIA, NATURELAND, and MEXICA. It is not uncommon in the SOUTHLANDS, and less common in the COMMERCIAL CORRIDOR and CONSERVATORY.

Beware classifying yourself into the technical-engineering-sales customer contact category if you have risen above this level, work on an important person's staff, or hold a position with a future in manufacturing or R and D. If the company perk car is like those used by the T-E-S group, drive something else. Something more like your boss, or even his boss. That's how you want your industry and competitors to classify you. It could make moving up a lot easier.

Company parking is another custom which should be dealt with cautiously.

In INDUSTRIA, in spite of union influence, many large plants still have separate parking lots for workers, skilled workers, foremen, and various classes of management. Where you are assigned to park is a clear, public statement of your corporate status.

Some, faced with this problem, take esoteric action. This is not advised. The ploy, for instance, of having someone drive you to work and drop you in the area designated for vice-presidents and above so you can walk to the office building and be seen coming from such an exalted parking lot, has disadvantages. You might unexpectedly need a car during the day to call upon a remote location. Seeking the loan of a vehicle from fellow employees is fine, once or twice. But if it happens too frequently, someone will discover your trick. You will find little future support.

In MEXICA, company parking is usually in a multi-story garage. It's not that there isn't ample land space for parking lots. It's that a garage provides shade. Parking under cover during much of the year is a quickly learned preference. In

April or May, not to mention August, the inside of a vehicle parked in the sun with all windows closed and doors locked can exceed 150 degrees. Dogs and babies trapped in cars have been known to expire in a matter of minutes. Obviously, if one is going to park and lock a car in direct sun, one should be sure no form of animal life is inside. Stories are told about double wrapping a pot roast in aluminum foil and leaving it on the dashboard against the windshield so as to gain a head start on dinner preparation. The garage in MEXICA is a status symbol in itself. A company spot anywhere, except on the roof, is prestigious.

An odd situation occurs in connection with company parking in NATURELAND. Automobiles are polluters. Polluting devices are not in favor amid clear-air/clean-living fanatics. Many corporate presidents belong to this school of thought, as do others on the executive tree.

With that background, examine the value of walking to work. Walking. Not riding public transport. There is no car in your designated spot. You are not a polluter. In fact, you are a physical fitness enthusiast—one of the best labels to have in NATURELAND. Rain or shine, it appears you walk to work. If called upon to perform a task requiring a vehicle, merely stroll a few blocks to where you've made clandestine arrangements to park. Some resourceful executives in the region make deals with homeowners near the office. For a pittance, they leave the car in front of the person's house during work.

When your business is through, park and walk back to the office. In any region but NATURELAND, you would be found out if your assignment took you three or four miles from your work station. In NATURELAND, a three or four mile hike sounds reasonable to those who live there.

In most of the COMMERCIAL CORRIDOR, concern over a company parking space is wasted worry. Until you attain exalted status, no parking is offered. In midtown Manhattan, you would have to be so exalted God himself would enquire if you needed tickets for grandstand viewing for The Second Coming.

More likely in New York is the use of a rental car at company expense. An advertising executive assigned to call on a client in New Jersey leaves the Manhattan office, walks to a rental car agency, picks up a previously reserved automobile, drives back to the office, loads the needed material and support staff, then makes the thirty mile drive. On returning, staff and stuff are dumped at the office, the car is driven to the rental firm, and the executive walks back to check calls. What would be a morning meeting in any other area becomes an all-day assignment in the COMMERCIAL CORRIDOR.

Notice the use of "reserved" in the above description? Rental car reservations are needed any day but are mandatory on Thursdays and Fridays because, without a reservation, there is no vehicle. Even with a reservation, the rental office which took the order may not have a car at its location. They will, however, be happy to use up to an hour of your time, not counting paperwork, to have a henchman drive you across town to another location where the vehicle you are assigned was returned.

Renting cars in other parts of the U.S. is not quite so traumatic. It is an act which generally occurs at the airport upon arrival. Return is usually made to the same location. Although in the VASTLANDS and WONDERLAND and NATURELAND, and to a lesser degree MEXICA, returning the vehicle to another agency a few hundred miles away is common (but more expensive). It's often, on trips of less than two hundred miles, about as quick to drive as it is to fight traffic to an airport and fly. Then again, many locations are not served by commercial air carrier. The highway is the only way.

Most companies have strict rules about the type of vehicle a manager may rent. In some, the higher the position, the more luxurious the car. Other organizations are not so stratified. The make and model is left to the discretion of the individual or charged against a total amount allotted for each day of travel, which includes transportation, food, lodging, and telephone.

Selecting the right rental car is important; the skill to drive it in the region, vital. Here are some regional comments.

IN THE CONSERVATORY:

Since it's impossible to rent a ten-year-old unit in pristine condition, follow the logic which makes such a car desirable and take the lowest-priced, cheapest-to-operate vehicle with a heater. If you can find one without a radio, so much the better. You won't enjoy it more, but you'll be appreciated for your sense of propriety; you'll make a good impression, and perhaps even enhance your career.

In Boston, rent at your own risk. Driving in Boston is not easy. That is an understatement. Driving in Boston for Bostonians, proper or not, is taxing. Driving in Boston for a non-Bostonian is a test of courage and nerve, not to mention navigational skills. Old-town narrow streets laid out on a grid seemingly designed by the artist M.C. Escher combine with a nonexistent "central artery" and an entirely original driver interpretation of traffic signal colors (green is go, yellow is go faster) to render the unknowing helpless. That's in good weather. A snowstorm during rush hour makes driving downright dangerous. Even suicidal. There is no purpose in admonishing caution. The situation is out of control the instant a stranger starts an engine. Let us not discuss parking. The only place it's worse comes next.

THE COMMERCIAL CORRIDOR:

If you fly into New York City or Philadelphia, do not rent. A limo is great for getting around and making impressions, but usually more expense than can be spread on the cheat sheet daily allowance.

Taxis are your best bet. Better in New York, best in Manhattan. If you have to rent, take something nondescript. See what they'll make a deal on. (What? You didn't know rental agencies make deals on some units? Where have you been? You must not travel much.)

Be sure, though, to obtain parking arrangements in advance if you are staying in either city. Through your hotel, if possible. Parking is *expensive*. Driving is a contest of conflicting wills.

THROUGHOUT THE SOUTHLANDS:

You'll have to rent. There is no public transportation to speak of, and in most places, a taxicab is a car used to run from hotels to the airport and not for inner-city transportation.

In New Orleans, no one cares what car you rent because downtown, everyone walks. There are several garages in the French Quarter which charge a troy ounce of gold per day per pound of car parked. Unless all your stops are downtown, though, you'll need a car. So, since nobody cares, rent a cheapie and use the saved cash for a good Creole dinner.

Atlanta is a little more car conscious than the rest of the region. It's better to move up to a midrange roller as opposed to the ultimate cheapo. No reason to go more than midrange.

In the rest of the SOUTHLANDS, ask what they've got and haggle over prices before deciding. Even if you've reserved a certain model, there may be a better local deal caused by competition. Shop a little. There is seldom so much demand all rental offices at an airport are sold out.

Rent a car one notch above what you drive at home. If you drive at home. If you don't have a car back home, think what a friend might drive, excluding foreign fast wheels. Then add a little to it. There is prestige in a car here. The upper midline can make you appear more certain of yourself and prosperous.

INDUSTRIA:

An interesting situation occurs among executives of major auto makers. When they travel, they rent the competition's cars, so they can compare their line to others in on-the-road conditions. Many actually make competitive reports back to the home office.

In this zone, rent an American vehicle, preferably one from the upper midrange to full-size range. Get a color other than blue, black, or white, at all costs. You don't want to look like one of the traveling tech reps. If in doubt go higher in cost. You'll be able to afford it because parking is included in the price of most hotel/motel rooms.

Drivers here are aggressive, especially at shift change times. Be particularly cautious near clusters of cars at bars.

HEARTLAND AMERICA:

Follow folk legend here which holds that a big car is safer. Do not discuss the fact that no one has ever proven same. Just go along with the party line and rent a big car in a conservative white or black. No bright reds, yellows, or other colors. Rent American. Look American. Drive American, too, which means, in this region, deliberately, but not fast. No tire squealing on starts or going around corners. Stay alert, though. This is the home of the faith lane changer—one who alters lanes at speed without looking to check if the new lane is occupied. Parking is no problem and is not, in comparison to the balance of the U.S., expensive. Even in Chicago.

Cautionary Notice for All Zones:

If you come from a place where there is no snow, ice, or frozen road surfaces to contend with, do not, repeat, do not get off a plane, into a car, and onto a frozen street or freeway. Everyone knows not to drive on freezing streets unless you are accustomed to doing so. Right? Wrong. Records show numerous accidents in Denver every winter caused by Sun Belters in town on business forgetting that 32 degrees is the freezing point of water.

If you are seasoned in cold-climate driving, use caution in the Sun Belt or far southern Florida in summer months. The road will be slicker than an eel on polished glass (a south Florida expression) if a light pattering of rain falls.

THE VASTLANDS:

Here we have mountains and deserts. Endless reaches of roads and, occasionally, endless roads that don't seem to reach anywhere.

Chances are, you can't rent a truck. If you can, do so. Even a mini pickup. It will mark you as one of the gang. Or at least someone who is trying.

Otherwise, go for a station wagon. No matter the only passenger will be you and the only business material needing transport is a sixteen-page contract. The wagon is status, if a truck isn't available.

A sedan, as a last resort, is adequate. Try for an import front-wheel drive. If you can find a four-wheel driver, so much the better.

Don't bother spending much for a rental car. The rental agency won't have anything which will impress anyone. And don't worry about parking. There's all the space in the world. Where you can, save your bucks for long neck beers or straight shooters of tequila in one of the more colorful bars. A night of executive drinking is expensive. VASTLANDers are proud of their liquor and charge accordingly.

NATURELAND:

Ideally, find the government report on automobile pollution and select the lowest polluter. Quote the statistics. Your business associates will realize they have come in contact with a kindred spirit and your dealing will be immensely easier.

If there is any question in your mind, take the smallest car possible, the same unit you'd select for the CONSERVA-TORY. The reasoning is different here, but the end model is identical. In NATURELAND, the smaller car takes up less space, burns less gas, and says "thoughtful conservationist" everywhere you drive it. That's a high accolade for this part of the world. One which will stand you in good stead.

Parking, outside of San Francisco where it is almost as bad as the worst places in the COMMERCIAL CORRI-DOR, is plentiful and cheap. It can also be entertaining. In Seattle, the fifty-story First National Bank Building has a different recorded tune playing outside the elevator at each parking level. Honest. Floor themes include "I Left My Heart in San Francisco," "New York, New York," "Kansas City," and, of course, "Seattle."

Be of good cheer. This is one of the lowest automotive cost zones in the U.S.

WONDERLAND:

There is no way on earth to rent an automobile too gaudy or too extreme for WONDERLAND use. Do not even try. There are many places offering exotics on short-term rental, but at the prices charged, you're better off hiring a car and driver. Not too shabby an idea, either, considering personal safety. This brings us to one of the most difficult-to-deal-with aspects of the WONDERLAND business community.

It is said "familiarity breeds contempt." This being the case, the California freeway system, to WONDERLAND executives, is contemptible.

Doing business in the area means driving on freeways. A lot of driving on freeways. California freeways do not run at posted speeds. They operate like light switches. One instant, vehicles are pressed toward terminal velocity. The next, all have stopped, or are puttering along at speeds comparable to a leisurely stroll. The untrained eye sees no cause for an abrupt alteration from allegro to andante, therefore often does not respond in time to make the needed change in tempo. This results in a collision, or at least a near miss. Near missers, not to mention colliders, are treated with disdain by those familiar with freeways. The higher the price of the vehicle driven by the disdainer, the more clearly the feeling is shown.

It is proper, if you are in WONDERLAND on a business mission, to drive by yourself on the freeway. Do not, under any circumstances, drive with a local business associate or prospect in the car. Do not even sit behind the steering wheel with such a passenger aboard.

Several excuses: "I don't know my way around"; "You drive, I'd like to see the scenery"; or "I left my pilot's license at home. Didn't know I'd be needing it," should be practiced in front of a mirror until they can be delivered with a convincing voice and earnest expression.

Why should you not drive with a native associate? Because that person's contempt for the freeway can, if you do not show an acceptable level of freeway virtuosity, be directed at you!

In WONDERLAND, where executive status is displayed by and locked to the automobile symbol, it is a matter of equal pride and prestige to be able to drive the automobile, as well. Driving means freeway motoring. Poor driving marks the driver as a cretin. Since less driving skill is expected in one piloting a Chevrolet than a Porsche, it is safer to stay away from two seat bolides and perch on the front bench of a family four banger. At least until you can manage an adequate level of freeway contempt through familiarity.

This is another reason the hired car and driver was suggested. You can remain in control of the vehicle, through the skilled hands of a chauffeur, who knows WONDERLAND like his or her lap, and still take business associates or clients about without fear of generating their distaste. It's worth considering.

Do not attempt to use public transportation in WON-DERLAND. Nothing goes when you need it or where you wish to be.

Company cars, as perks, hit the big time in WONDER-LAND, then began to fade as the IRS became stingy in allowances for style. The leased vehicle seems in for a long reign. An executive leases the car and the company increases salary or allows greater expense account use to offset all or part of the cost. The executive writes off the use of the vehicle in business; the company does not have the added burden of vehicle ownership, not to mention liability; and the IRS is pleased because it has prevented a loss of coin to government coffers. That, by the way, is a typical WONDER-LAND business arrangement. Everyone gets a bit of what he/she wants and all appear to be winners.

One additional comment on WONDERLAND. Returning cars to most airport rental agencies is not pleasant. In Los Angeles it can become a time-consuming horror. Far better to drop the vehicle at a hotel rental agency and take a cab to the airport. The sanity you save may be your own.

A final note. Do not worry about parking. WONDER-LAND is built on the automobile. Without ample, inexpensive parking, it wouldn't exist.

MEXICA:

The variety of automobiling in MEXICA is exceeded only by that of WONDERLAND.

Rent according to your travel needs: a smaller model about town; a larger, faster unit for long distances on the road.

Drive carefully. Others (read "natives") do not. Inherent in the macho philosophy is commitment toward fulfillment of immediate desires. This can have frightening ramifications in motoring.

Example: You are driving on a two-lane road. (There are lots of two-lane roads in MEXICA.) You are in a sandstorm. (There are lots of sandstorms in MEXICA.) You can't see ahead. (Lots of people in MEXICA cannot see any farther than their chins.)

You are in the midst of a long line of cars. Ten ahead, ten or more behind, all with lights shining in the blowing gloom. Cars pass from the other direction, headlamps dull bright spots. Your vehicle shakes as they speed by. Wind is making so much noise you can barely hear the radio. Out the window, the weather is so bad you see birds walking alongside the road. Birds walking says it all.

Somewhere ahead, the lead car slows as the driver's vision is momentarily blocked. There is a brief blare of horn, and from behind you, a car detaches itself from your line, snaps into the oncoming lane, and accelerates madly. The driver hangs in the wrong lane for an impossibly long time, his red taillights getting smaller, then swings back, becoming the new leader of your string. A second later, three huge eighteen-wheel tractor-trailer rigs, nose to tail, whip past. Had the unknown driver waited a heartbeat longer before pulling in, there would have been blood on the highway.

Question: What sex was the driver of the passing car?

Answer: Male. Only males can be macho, remember?

What does macho have to do with attempted suicide? Everything. And nothing. The driver was not trying to kill himself. He was merely responding to a macho urge, which held that he would rather be dead than trapped where he was another instant. Naturally, with that commitment, he pulled out and passed. Had he been killed, it would not have been suicide. His pride/honor/peace of mind was saved by acting. Had death ensued, so be it.

Think about the motivation for a moment. He would rather be dead than where he was. If other people were killed through his action, that was of no matter to him. He could not remain where he was any longer.

That philosophy applies to business as well as driving. It's another regional concept to remember.

So, in MEXICA, rent anything and drive carefully.

Someone else will take care of recklessness for you. Watch the speed limit; add five miles per hour to posted speeds. Police (many, many more than you will be accustomed to seeing in any other region) have declared an unofficial amnesty range between 5 and 10 miles per hour over the 55 limit. Stay there, even though you see drivers tearing along at 80 and 90. They have merely decided they'd rather be ticketed than go any slower. Macho in action, again.

Finally, parking is not a worry. A few of the big cities have dense traffic (Houston, Dallas, and Phoenix), but there are outdoor surface parking lots even in the heart of central business districts. In smaller towns, meters abound, as do free lots. WONDERLAND was built on the automobile and would fail if drivers couldn't park, dismount, and conduct business. In this regard, at least, MEXICA equals its more flamboyant neighbor.

A word more about Houston. Manhattan crosstown traffic is fast moving and orderly compared to Houston freeways during rush hours. Rush hours run from 6:00 A.M. to noon, and from noon to 6:00 P.M. Then evening traffic jams begin.

Natural forward creep imparted to a car from an automatic transmission is called the Houston Freeway Gear. As long as the air conditioner and radio work, most Houstonians, inured to the situation, hold their tempers. Many also carry guns in their cars. If unairconditioned vehicles ever make a comeback, there will be murder on the freeways of Astrodome City.

WASHINGTON, D.C.:

Washington is, like the other Eternal City, Rome, in a state of eternal gridlock. Traffic does not jam in Washington. It stops. For unpredictably long periods of time. If you have to drive, drive anything. But get full insurance coverage, and if the rental agency will sell you a rider to increase your limits, take that, too.

Transportation in Washington proper is adequate. Review your schedule, find out if any of your associates can drive you, and skip renting a car if you can. It's a long haul to Dulles from the area around the Capitol and the trip costs in a taxi. But chances are, the driver knows the way and you'll get there. On time and in one piece.

Parking is another difficulty. In the summer, when every family loads up the old jalopy and rolls into town, parking becomes as scarce as wanted kidnappers at an FBI convention. Save yourself. Call out personal favors on your associates. Don't rely on friends because they change so quickly in Foggy Bottom.

MIAMI:

For Miami, don't do it. Don't rent. Pay to ride a cab. Although they're not easy to find, you'll be glad you did. It is hard driving for yourself; there is no parking to speak of, and many places you can park, you wouldn't, for fear of personal assault on your health or wealth. It's not so bad if you speak Spanish. That can help. Even so, the place is a nightmare for the first-time visiting business executive. Auto theft must be a course taught in school; teenagers have probably formed social clubs centered on the activity.

If you do rent, take anything insurable. Then, as in Washington, insure for as much as you can. If all you bring back is the key and a hubcap you found in the space you parked, you want no liability.

There are two additional automobile-related regional differences in the business community. The first has to do with styles of driving.

The three main styles are:

A. Business person in isolated, deep thought.

B. Business persons in animated conversation.

C. Business persons in group silence.

Each of these conditions brings out a regional display worthy of note.

In the VASTLANDS, NATURELAND, and WONDER-LAND, business person alone in thought is frequently accompanied by moving lips as the executive verbalizes thoughts. Talking aloud while alone is not seen as talking to oneself. Lips move in the COMMERCIAL CORRIDOR, too, but even an inexperienced lip-reader can see blasphemies and unkind names being repeated in response to aggressive driving demonstrations or impaired speed of cross-flow traffic.

Talking to yourself while driving is acceptable behavior in the above zones. It should not be done in the SOUTH-LANDS, as someone will observe mouth motion and believe you are Biblically inspired, speaking in tongues. You may find it hard to keep friends with your growing reputation for religious extremism.

Talking to yourself while driving in HEARTLAND AMERICA will rapidly mark you as an untrustworthy eccentric. It is, however, highly acceptable to sing country and western lyrics along with a performer on the radio.

Talking to yourself in the CONSERVATORY is not a good idea at all, as the practice smacks of possession and we all know what happens to witches in that part of America.

Business persons inside a traveling car in animated conversation with each other, as long as it is not acrimonious debate, is common throughout the SOUTHLANDS, IN-DUSTRIA (although for other reasons), the VASTLANDS, NATURELAND, and MEXICA.

It is not common in WONDERLAND, where everyone has his/her own car and wouldn't be seen dead in yours. Besides, there is apparently a law banning the use of a motor vehicle by more than two consenting adults, as one never sees carloads of business people anywhere.

In Washington, as on elevators, a seat in any car is the signal to begin nonstop talking and nonstart listening.

In Miami, all the people in the car talk constantly, to themselves and each other. The only problem is they speak Spanish.

INDUSTRIA areas carpool tech reps, sales reps, union reps, and every other rep known to man. All that's required is a common city destination. Akron, Ohio, say. (Akron is like Detroit, without the glitter.) After checking into a hotel, each goes a separate way. All will meet at a prearranged time and carpool back to home base. In the auto all talking is confusion. The sales people don't understand what the tech reps are saying, the tech folks couldn't care less about sales concerns, the union reps hold out for equal time, and everyone gets along just fine. The car, in short, becomes a microcosm of corporate structure.

Talk in the VASTLANDS concerns business, but often also ranges to social chitchat. Population is so scant two people don't meet often enough to get much chance to palaver. When the opportunity arises, it is taken with gusto.

Groups in NATURELAND spend hours discussing how things were before the coming of the white man and agreeing on how lucky they all are to live in the Garden of Unspoiled Eden. Business is discussed as a sideline only. There are more important issues to those who are one with the mountains.

Group talk in MEXICA is an Anglicized version of the Miami scene. Border Mexican is not Spanish, however. It is spoken more slowly, has an intrusion of English words and phrases, and is accented in a certain stylistic way. If the group is speaking English, there will be a combination of western taciturnity and southern enthusiasm. Business is the only subject, in any case, as getting into personal details with someone while part of a group flirts with public display of emotions.

If a gaggle of business people is detected riding in silence in any region, the scene should be observed with care. Either they are not business executives or they are recovering from a traumatic shared experience. Real business people always confer when they get together. Especially if there are no telephones or reports to read. Silence is an anathema to the breed. What is said does not have to make sense. Much of business is conducted on the basis of nonsense, as any honest manager will testify. If you run across the phenomenon of business people riding in silence, unless they are overcome by scenic beauty (a not infrequent occurrence in NATURELAND), watch the business press for the next few days. A disaster of a size to cause such silence is sure to make headlines.

The final point of automotive discussion deals with parking on private lots in conjunction with business meetings or meals.

Those business people in New York and Philadelphia may not fully appreciate the protocol problems found in such a simple act as driving in and leaving your vehicle with the lot attendant. These comments will point out some regional variances.

One cardinal rule holds in all zones. The driver must look assured. A confident appearance breeds internal confidence. Drive in as if you belong. Even if you know you don't.

Readers please note: Parking in some areas requires more panache than others. By this point in our discussion, it should be clear which is which. Please use your imagination, now, before reading any further, and administer the following self-test:

Q: Which areas require the most parking lot panache?

A: Any place in WONDERLAND. Followed by any location in MEXICA, if you are driving a brand new or very expensive vehicle. Attitude is paramount. You must not look as if the car you drive impresses you in the least.

Q: Which areas require a low key approach?

A: INDUSTRIA and HEARTLAND, especially if you are driving a new or very expensive vehicle.

Q: Where is worrying about a public parking lot not a problem?

A: New York and Houston. In New York, there are none, or almost none, and if you find one, it will be full. Do not be put off by the "Full" sign. A buck or so to an attendant will create a space. If it doesn't, they really are full. And you are probably out a buck or so.

In Houston, where blocks of privately owned downtown land are used for open-air parking lots, your concern is how near you'd like to be to your final destination. In the summer, park near. Heat in the streets is past description.

How did you score? Five points for each correct answer. You should have gotten fifteen. Nothing less is acceptable.

In New York, be certain the parking attendant who takes your car is indeed a certified attendant, not a thief. More than one suburban couple, in the city for a night on the town, has pulled in front of a restaurant, been helped from their Mercedes, given a claim chit, and assisted to the door, only to discover, at the end of a meal a few hours later, the establishment has no valet parking. Thorough thieves have gone to the trouble of printing up claim tickets and even having a folding "Valet Parking" sign painted.

In the Inland South, check to be certain your hand brake is off before handing your vehicle to a lot attendant, lest he or she drive the car without noticing the added drag, the elevated rear end, or unusual noises from under the body.

In MEXICA, insist on having your car parked close by. Those far from light on a dark night may have parts taken to add inventory to the Midnight Auto Supply Company.

In WONDERLAND, MEXICA, and the SOUTH-LANDS, always, repeat, always tip the lot attendant when he/she takes your car. A tip up front is like a stitch in time.

For WONDERLAND use only: tear a five dollar bill down the middle, give half to the attendant, take the claim check, and walk away. Naturally, the parker gets the other half when you leave.

Tipping up front implies a second gratuity on the back-side of the transaction when your car is brought to you. If you don't like the way it has been driven, drive off. But take care driving back again if the same attendant is present.

Overall, when traveling, remember: How you live on the road will be taken by associates and clients as the equivalent of how you conduct yourself at home. The right car can and will offset other economies because the car is highly visible. A lot of penny-pinching can be hidden. The right vehicle, in tune with regional attitudes, will compensate for other errors in behavior. And help you make a good first impression.

CHAPTER

6

OFFICE
OBSERVATIONS

Space planning, utilization,
style, and ducks

Across the country, office prestige follows a general rule. The more exalted the position, the larger the office. Absolute size varies, however. In the COMMERCIAL CORRIDOR, space allotted per person is less than in NATURELAND. Rent rates per square foot are partially the cause of the difference, but other factors are at work. These include size of competitor's space, size of client's facilities, the likelihood of visitors on premises, and management attitudes toward ostentatious display.

Decor of offices is another variable with clear regional overtones. For the purposes of this chapter, decor is furniture and overall look of the office. In many companies this is a dictated constant that will not vary from department to department or from site to site.

Personal accessories, those peculiar items an individual brings into an office, usually representing an interest or an indication of lifestyle, also provide grounds for study.

A quick regional run-through will cover size and decor.

CONSERVATORY:

As in almost all things, this region is consistent with its traditions. In the case of office furniture, it has produced a standard.

Sturdy desks and chairs, of no particular manufacture or design distinction, bought when the firm was founded in 1829, have, through use and passage of time, become antiques. So the office, originally furnished plainly to show the solidity of the organization, is now a classic tastemaker, fitted out in New England antiquities. Those firms not fortunate enough or staunch enough to have lasted a hundred or more years feel their lack and wish to look as if they have. So they pay exorbitant prices to antique dealers for what was, until the 1960s, used office furniture.

Tradition also determines the amount of space—as little as possible. In the days before central heating, when a smoldering fireplace gave light and kept a scum of ice from forming on top of ink wells, economy dictated a single work room. Since each enclosed space had to have a separate fire, and each fire cost money each moment it burned, one room meant one fire and subsequent lower operations costs. One room also meant no talking, so others could concentrate on their work. The advent of the telephone intruded into this simple arrangement, but was cared for in a similarly plain manner. No one put in business telephones until the demands of the world forced them.

The one-room concept, however, still remains. Not only can more bodies be crammed into a space, there is no waste from square inches being taken up by the thickness of walls. Separate offices are allowed only for the masters of the premises. And their accountant, to preserve confidentiality of the finances and operations.

Large corporations from outside that move in to do business have broken with tradition. Taking space in newer buildings, many with elevators instead of stairs to trod, these companies have spoiled their workers by often having as few as two or three in a single work area. Their look is of plastic and pastels as opposed to dingy-cream walls and natural wood covered with ageless grime.

To those who know, however, the typical CONSERVA-TORY office is a place for work, not appreciation of view or the disturbing influence of color. Solid individuals work for solid firms, companies with proven survival abilities and with reputations for practical efficiency.

In this context, a partner's office is just that. An office. Not a museum or place for untoward display of personal taste or experience. An office, by God! An office!

So it always has been. So it always should be. So it certainly shall be.

COMMERCIAL CORRIDOR:

Nowhere in America does one see such an astounding variation in office space as displayed by accommodations in this zone.

Rent is a major overhead item in every operation. In the COMMERCIAL CORRIDOR, rent often becomes *the* overhead factor.

Throughout the area is an appreciation for quality offices located in bright, new, airy space, with good views, and complimented by the best designer furniture and furnishings. Color is revered for wall surfaces, and floor coverings are selected to highlight the positive influences that flow from the right kind of surroundings.

This attitude is remarkable. All the more so because office space, as it is actually used, borders too often on the deplorable.

Even those businesses engaged in creative pursuits, like major advertising agencies, are housed in facilities that would be considered drab and featureless in many other zones. Regardless of strong feelings about wanting good space, the costs, coupled to an unstated agreement with competitors not to let building owners take in profits that would have gone to the business, dictate otherwise. Mundane offices, furnished with durable metal desks and chairs, are the rule. Bright spots are exceptions. But even here, if one is allowed to look behind the facade intended to confront visitors, too little of the style is carried throughout the facilities.

There are some stunning offices in the COMMERCIAL CORRIDOR. They are the exceptions and stand out all the more for that distinction. Most companies operate in space that can be called adequate. Crowding of work stations is normal, privacy limited, and corridors minimal. Even chief-executive sanctuaries are smaller than counterparts in other areas of the U.S.

Combine this attitude toward the work place with control of as much American business as is managed by leaders in the COMMERCIAL CORRIDOR, and the far-reaching effects of this style bias can be fully appreciated.

It's a case of knowing better, and even perhaps wanting better, but not being willing to pay for it.

SOUTHLANDS:

Atlantic Coast. Picture a low- to mid-rise building with narrow windows, surrounded by more of the same. If that's not the region's ideal, it's the reality. Offices here share with the rest of the SOUTHLANDS, excepting Atlanta, a late 1950s look. They differ with the other two Souths only in terms of business tradition.

Influences here have been less agricultural and more commercial. Especially in the area of transporting goods, which has brought about an interchange of ideas with those from other parts of the U.S. and the world. This broadening process is seen in much of the office space, which sports an appearance closer to the COMMERCIAL CORRIDOR than

Inland or Gulf South zones. New glass and concrete high-rise buildings are appearing, but usually as bank headquarters. Office space is in good supply so rent rates aren't totally oppressive. This leads to freer use of space and less jamming of people.

There is clearly a regional effect at work in the question of space allotted per employee. Crowded work conditions match crowded streets and crowded public areas. Lessen the population, and space allocated per person increases in almost direct proportion.

Atlantic South office space reflects the lifestyle: traditional, genteel, and gracious, with nothing gaudy. A sufficiency of room for everyone, but nothing so exceptionally spacious as to generate unseemly comment. A good building, but not a new building. The choice of convenient location over fashionable address. Enough, but never too much.

ATLANTA:

The inclination in taste along the COMMERCIAL CORRIDOR for lavish, well-composed, bright offices has found free rein in the steel, glass, and concrete high rises that cover the three main Atlanta business districts. Rental rates allow taking ample space to house staff and leave room for niceties that come only from sufficient square footage to arrange and create. Even open work areas for clerical employees provide privacy and allow concentration. Upper level executives' offices are larger than found in the CORRIDOR or the SOUTHLANDS. They almost always sport a fine view and usually feature built-in cabinets. Separate work and conference areas are the norm.

Atlanta still has buildings akin to the Inland South, but more and more of the organizations owned or operated by those outside the city are taking new facilities to satisfy unfulfilled desires of COMMERCIAL CORRIDOR executives for power offices.

THE INLAND SOUTH:

Major cities have high-rise, glass-sided towers placed adjacent to medium-rise older masonry buildings with gargoyles and other symbols of a long-gone architectural age.

Smaller towns have three- and four-story construction housing the same type offices, furnished in much the same way as the users of medium-rise space in the city. This indicates that at one time, there was little rural-urban difference in space or furniture. Times are changing, yet a noticeable differential in office style is only recently apparent. This will have other effects on the progressive splitting of the business community in this zone.

Only the most adventurous firms dare show their tastes through the portions of office space open for public view. Those that do, however, demonstrate levels of imagination and space utilization which would be right at home in WONDERLAND. Business offices in the Inland South are in a period of change. For the better.

THE GULF SOUTH:

Low-medium rises predominate. Tampa has moved rapidly toward clean steel and glass construction, replacing much of the central business district with new, bright, airy office space. A couple of other cities are following suit. Overall, though, available space is rather drab. It is, however, priced to allow for enough room.

As the Atlantic Ocean's climate and presence brings something perceivable to the cities lining its shore, the Gulf of Mexico's influence can be felt in this sector. Hurricanes are an annual event, as is flooding from intense tropical downpours and unending days of steamy sunshine. There is a strong outdoor feeling here reflected in the buildings. Windows are wider than in the COMMERCIAL CORRIDOR, setbacks on lots are deeper, and there is a more human feeling to the space.

Furniture and furnishings follow the southern trend. Either it's new, a decade or less since purchase, and made of heavy wood or metal in rather square shapes, or it's old, dating to the 1920s. Old furniture is not better looking than new, as neither was intended for entry in a design competition. It is durable stuff, of no particular visual interest. An occasional rolltop desk is seen, but the partner's desk, so favored in the CONSERVATORY, is not popular here. Southern independence seems to demand one executive in one office. Rent rates and space availability combine to allow it, so the practice will prove a hard one to discontinue.

INDUSTRIA:

Offices in INDUSTRIA are generally utilitarian, and often built as part of a manufacturing facility. Main cities sport modern high rises, but area-wise, more square footage is still available in older buildings.

Smaller towns have space for banks and service companies, but the greatest portion of commercial space outside large cities is sited in plant locations.

In truth, most offices are rather drab. It may be that engineers appreciate static space. Or that engineers pride themselves on making do with what they have. In either case, because there are so many engineers in this zone, it seems to be a place for efficient spaces as opposed to luxurious surroundings. Better meeting rooms are decorated in early Hilton Hotel, making full use of folding tables and stackable chairs. Those are the better ones; there's no use mentioning the average and below.

Considering that automobile manufacturing companies are some of the largest businesses in America, one might expect better executive quarters. Their space, overall, while old, is in good repair. When the buildings were constructed, many did not include central climate control. Heating, yes. Cold air, no. That's been added later.

Older construction is handsomely roomy, with wide corridors and natural wood door frames. There is a fishbowl feeling with the amount of glass used to close off individual offices from corridors. In a way, it's a holdover from a traditional business practice of having supervisors look in, literally, on workers. The need may still be present, in some cases, but modern management styles no longer approve of such obvious techniques.

Understand, too, that auto companies have built recent quarters which rival the best commercial space in any city. Also, that the upper echelon of executives is housed quite well indeed. But also know that new structures are only a small part of their total space mix.

The less said about offices at plant sites the better. Esthetically, there is an impression that offices, like assembly lines or other manufacturing systems for which the plant exists, are the same. There is a sterile atmosphere which, once experienced, isn't forgotten. Attempts at adding pictures and carpet fall short of the desired effect. The hard-edged furniture looks okay, if your taste runs to gunmetal-gray sheet steel and green vinyl.

HEARTLAND AMERICA:

Let's start with Chicago. There is one area of the city, inside the loop, where high-rise buildings offer the most modern of accommodations. This is affected by high rents, of course, so space utilization (which always means cramming more people into less room and diminishing key dimensions) is heavily practiced.

Chicago, like New York and a few other cities where huge structures are erected in the central business district, suffers from the constraint of land cost. This makes for large floors in new buildings. When floor size exceeds fifteen thousand square feet, and there is management pressure to provide as many work stations as possible, an entire cluster of offices is going to be forced to open onto a hallway and have no outside exposure. Large floors result in a core that must be used.

On smaller floors, central space can accommodate computer installations and conference rooms. Once floor size increases, humans are going to be housed away from daylight. It's a tough decision for management, but you can bet it won't be the executive cadre missing sunshine.

The curse of Chicago, New York City, Philadelphia, San Francisco, and other major metro areas is age, resulting in a mix of very old office space and very new. Or, said another way, very bad space and very good space.

Back to Chicago. Companies have offices that are fabulous and offices that are a fate worse than death. Often the same company has both, in two different locations.

Bright, well-lit, new skyscraper space goes with the latest Hermann Miller and Knoll creations. Dark, dingy, and decrepit fit naturally with the stolid oak uglies of the 1950s.

In terms of office space, Chicago has a split personality where, unlike New York, the building dictates the atmosphere and furniture of the organization. It's as if no one thought of brightening older space to make it more attractive.

The balance of HEARTLAND AMERICA is absolutely destitute when it comes to nice office space. Someone will read this and take exception, because he/she has the one office in a thousand which is well furnished and sited in a graceful building. As a rule, offices here have the aged feeling of a 1940s radio soap opera. Some employees resemble characters from those dramas.

VASTLANDS:

Office space in the VASTLANDS runs from Denver Redone or Denver New to Salt Lake Traditional. What little space there is—apart from offices located at mines, in trailers at oil sites, in logging camps, or belonging to the U.S. Forest Service—is utilitarian. Furnishings are 1960 Army or Danish Cheap.

Not a lot to say about office space or furniture in the VASTLANDS. There is so little of it. And so little of that done well. Some private organizations, such as Johns-Manville outside Denver, are unique. The company did its own building and made a distinctive statement. Pity this is the exception, not the norm.

NATURELAND:

The NATURELAND executive would like to have an office in a log cabin on a forested island. And not just any log cabin—one built without nails and with bark still on the logs.

Instead, most executives are housed in short-rise buildings showing their age. A few take the taller glass and steel newcomers, but most make do with space built in the days of their fathers and not improved much since.

Furniture fits the need and philosophy. Steel desks, tables, and chairs. Making office furniture from wood seems almost sacrilegious. At home there is wood furniture, but it is beautifully finished and cared for. Offices use plastic and/or steel. That keeps the pollutants in the MEXICA petrochemical belt and in INDUSTRIA well away from NATURE-LAND proper.

As an aside, the nationwide use of steel desks, chairs, etc. would seem to result in a similarity between offices in different locales. In truth, it does. On the surface. Reasons for selecting the furniture, its placement in rooms, condition, and the space itself give variety. More, differences are divisible by our zones and show the personality of each zone quite clearly.

WONDERLAND:

Even a crummy office here is not as crummy as it would be if it were located in the COMMERCIAL CORRIDOR or IN-DUSTRIA. There are some crummy offices in WONDER-

LAND and the motion picture industry rents most of them. Movie executives and managers are accustomed to less than opulent work surroundings. Studio accommodations are and have often been remodeled trailers, so everyone has developed a taste for marginal quarters. Older buildings, which rent by the week and allow a producer to have five full floors three months, then a thousand-square-foot office for the balance of the year, thus meeting staff needs while making a thirteen-week TV series, are serviceable. Executive homes are lavish; executive offices usually are not.

Outside the motion picture-TV industry, better space is used. But with few exceptions, the impact of the attitude toward office space spawned by movie moguls dulls the blithe WONDERLAND spirit, stifling an otherwise insatiable urge for the gaudy and bizarre.

There are nice offices. There are only a few older buildings, which may be why producers treasure them so dearly. Overall, though, less attention is paid to office surroundings than to personal dress, jewelry, or driving machines.

MEXICA:

Because of geographic diversity, businesses are often housed in a two-room combo up one flight of worn wooden stairs in a red brick building across Main Street from the train station. The other extreme is found in the new high-rise crystal towers in Houston or Dallas that have replaced much of the earlier construction and are built in clusters bigger than many small towns.

Different types of businesses take different attitudes toward space requirements. Part of this is practical, part regionally oriented, and part attitudinally aligned with tradition. In MEXICA, the practice is strongly ingrained.

Take banks, for instance. MEXICA bankers, as much or more than counterparts found in other areas, crave impressive lobby and reception areas, and use these spaces as facades to cover a multitude of rather small cubical offices. Expansive public areas are used to present an aura of success and prestige. Tiny offices house those workers who must have privacy to do their jobs.

Law firms love to show good taste through lavishly decorated office space, although they too are forced, because of the number of people who need privacy, to build corridors of small offices broken by the more spacious partner's suites. Knowledgeable law firms also display their libraries to visitors. The sight of so many law books is intimidating, but reassuring.

Accounting firms follow the same pattern, as their needs parallel those of their legal cousins. They also use a plethora of dinky offices.

Major firms doing business in the oil patch say to hell with all that and make everyone's office big, and the upper echelon's space spacious. If large public areas are good, then good is not enough. They make them bigger. If the tasteful mid-priced furniture used by the money changers, mouth pieces, and bean counters is acceptable in its polished wooden glory, they go 'em one better. It's glass and steel and teak and burnished chrome. Do large floors force central cores of windowless offices? Certainly not. Just make the offices bigger and store something in what's left of the middle after corridors large enough to drive cattle through are placed to connect everyone with everything.

Even in smaller towns and the oil patch offices located in hundreds of pipe yards, rig yards, supply yards, mud centers, etc., or what cannot be handled through refinement of structure is compensated for through use of size. The rule seems to be: when you think there is enough space, double it.

Some executives in oil patch companies have exquisite taste, as is shown by their suites, jet interiors, and the general look of their company quarters. Others present a crass opulence as tasteless as it is nonsensical. In either case, oil patch management feels strongly about appearing in a certain fashion to friends, clients, and employees.

Outside the oil patch, away from the larger cities, MEXICA business facilities run from grim to ghastly. In practice, a little of the CONSERVATORY's use of antiques is apparent and comes from the same cause. It's the furniture that has been in the office for decades.

Surprisingly, some of the fast growth urban areas (San Antonio, San Diego, and Phoenix) have undergone a revitalization of the central business district, led mostly by banks seeking to make a community statement by participation in the development of a high rise.

There is a consistent tendency, because of increased rental rates, to place more individuals in a given work area than efficiency dictates. In many instances, this results in buildings that are stylish outside, but crammed and jammed on every floor.

WASHINGTON, D.C.:

The Government Look, a uniform display of equality pervading federal offices, intrudes into those companies which do business with the government. Blandness of furnishings, coupled with a sense of temporary residence in the building, combine to produce an office environment as sanitary and homelike as an Air Force barracks or Navy ship in the North Sea. Warm it is not.

Furniture and office machines are issued from a huge central government stockpile. One takes what one gets.

The force of federal style pervades the business community in this area, and aside from a few law firms, which cater to the refined, expensive tastes of clients wealthy enough to employ them, monotonous sameness is the rule. No one notices. The government doesn't wish to give taxpayers an impression of money spent on glamor or gewgaws. Neither do major government contractors who follow the federal lead. Since offices are consistent throughout the District of Columbia and environs, it works rather like school uniforms on children. There is no need to strive for designer clothes as they can't be worn where it counts. Those who must succumb to the urge for personal decoration do so at their own peril. It's the system. And in school, in business, or in Washington, it can be difficult to buck the system.

MIAMI:

In Miami, most office space is a little run-down. Even in the new buildings. Most of the individuals renting space come to Miami from places where "a little run-down" is terrific. Latins, including Cubans (who tend to behave in a highly unLatin fashion), are accustomed to buildings which look unfinished and more than "a little run-down" when brand new.

Armed with an appreciation of some of the most important regional attitudes toward office space, two more subjects can be pursued in a more general fashion.

Office decor, aside from strictures posed by overall corporate policy, is an area in which individual taste of the executive can play a role. The way an office or work station is personalized through accessories is expressive of individual regional attitudes.

Before passing onto this topic, though, one trend, seen in the COMMERCIAL CORRIDOR and INDUSTRIA, waxes and wanes through Big Corporation America.

There is no question office size equates to status in an organization. Likewise, the more expensive the furniture and accessories, the higher the rank of individual occupying the space.

It took a giant corporation's deluded controller to get proper control of these two obvious truths and, with the nearly

inhuman analysis often performed by some corporate accountants, devise a plan which relegates the status-office relationship to written company policy.

This type of formal rank-space plan is not widely seen
outside the COMMERCIAL CORRIDOR and INDUSTRIA,
except in branch offices of the larger companies that are
headquartered there. Why? Because in many areas, businesses must pay at least lip service to the managerial spirit
of equality. Many other firms have set rank-office policies in
full effect, but the requirements are not written. Unwritten
rules are made for self-enforcement.

Back to the subject of regionality in office decor. VAST-
LANDS, naturally, is inclined toward rough and ready. Indian art, western art, and firearms are all in demand and considered to be in impeccable executive taste. A gun rack, or
better still, a lockable gun cabinet with drawers for different
types of shells and cleaning equipment, is classic. Many executives here would be ecstatic over a work place that looked
like a cowtown sheriff's office in a technicolor western.

NATURELAND executives want windows. Preferably with
a view of mountains, forest, or water. Even on gray days (not
infrequent in NATURELAND), natural beauty overshadows
any artificial adornment humankind can manufacture and place
on the wall.

Photographs, showing more of the same scenery, or close-
up shots of animals, are also popular. These gain in prestige
if they are displayed in the office of the person who took
them. Even more prestige is gained if that individual also
did the darkroom work. Please understand, though, it is not
the photographic expertise that merits praise. What is appreciated is the ability to care for one's needs and the mastering
of another life-skill.

Display of personal effects is fine, especially if these are
pictures of man, wife, and children loaded with gear, back-
packing through a high mountain meadow or fishing. You get
the idea.

Windows are important in WONDERLAND, too. But for a different reason. In WONDERLAND, the window, preferably high above the city, looks out over automobiles and people: the two ingredients which make up so many fascinating possibilities for profit.

Taste in MEXICA, outside the oil patch, has ascended from pictures of matadors and bulls painted in fluorescent colors on black velvet. But not much. Some fine western art is found, and in the oil patch, there is a dementia for photos of oil rigs at sunset. It must be a symbol of money or hope. Either way, it is a popular motif, seen throughout the region and widely reproduced on calendars, which are valued as gifts.

In the COMMERCIAL CORRIDOR, as well as parts of the CONSERVATORY, there is a most unusual cult which seems to pay homage to the subfamily *Anatinae*, commonly, but mistakenly, called ducks. Properly, only the female of this group is a "duck." The male is a "drake." A fact which seems to concern no one, including those who are so involved with the creatures. Entire companies exist for the production of every article known to man imprinted with a picture of a duck. Artists spend their creative lives painting duck after duck after drake. Dozens more make careers of illustrating hunters shooting ducks, dogs with sheepish eyes retrieving ducks just shot, ducks flying into the air from water or behind logs, and men with guns and canvas vests (interesting that some canvaslike fabrics are known as "duck") carrying strings of dead birds.

Admiration bordering upon worship of the *Anatinae* class must be tinged with gloom, as the most common English expression dealing with these creatures is "dead duck."

Duck fancy seems to be part of Ivy League tradition. It is also interwoven into the folk ethic of the CONSERVATORY. Once an executive is smitten by a degenerative craving for duck images, there is apparently no cure. Office space suddenly blooms with ducks of every plumage and of every color. There are duck prints, pictures, pencils, desk decorators, paperweights, wallpapers, lapel pins, phone covers, letterheads, embossments on file cabinets, ties, jacket linings, lamps, lamp shades, staplers, and hundreds of other items, some too gruesome to imagine.

The duck fetish is especially fascinating because, although there are scattered outbreaks of it in San Francisco, Dallas, Houston, Washington, D.C., Richmond, and Atlanta, the real fever is contained in the CORRIDOR and CONSERVATORY. As might be expected, the cases afield from these regions can usually be traced to an individual who became infected while going to college or working in contaminated zones.

Ducks, while bizarre, are not the only items showing peculiar executive preference. Other "classic" regional displays include framed reproductions of Currier and Ives illustrations in the CONSERVATORY, hand-stamped Morocco leather desk sets (including matching leatherbound blotter, leather-scabbarded scissors, and a leather-wrapped pencil holder—all in red, green, or black with gold relief) in the COMMERCIAL CORRIDOR, and the aforementioned VASTLANDS' firearms display.

No executive office in the SOUTHLANDS can be considered complete without at least one family photograph. For those married, or divorced with children, pictures will focus on wife and kids, or kids alone. Childless couples must be content with pictures of themselves together, studio shots of each mate alone, or both mates and pet dog. Unmarrieds display photos of parents and, sometimes, their entire family, including brothers, sisters, father, mother, grandparents, uncles, aunts, cousins, and neighbors.

Snapshots, suitably framed and out of focus as amateur exposures generally are, seem highly personal but are displayed proudly. It makes no difference that the men in the family groupings all appear to have a snootfull, grinning inanely, heads at unusual angles to their bodies.

An abundance of these clan photos, combined with plentiful displays of wives, husbands, and children, have created an intriguing opening for conversation.

"How old's your boy?" said with a nod toward the photo, warms the heart, spurs a response, and is safe ground. It is an accepted ploy, allowing for the response, "Ten." The riposte to this would be: "They sure grow up quick." Or, if there is a desire to exchange confidences: "Ten. Mine's a little older. Twenty-one. Out of college and not Daddy's little girl anymore." This must be said in a tone which indicates wistful thoughts of times past, not regret that the girl has run away with a Spanish dancer and is living in a gypsy cave outside Sevilla.

In MEXICA, photos of family also play a vital role. Some go so far as to display children's pictures, but most do not. Men, however, show off a studio portrait of their wife or girlfriend. Never both. These color photographs, posed carefully using a drape across the shoulders, are a guide to the owner's prestige. First level is demonstrated by having such a photograph at all. Mere possession separates the executive from the have-nots, those individuals without the wherewithal or desire to spend a hundred bucks for a first class photographic sitting.

Second level is determined by the status of the photographer whose name is emblazoned in an upper or lower corner of the print. Masters of the pecking order instantly recognize the signature or symbol of the top ten most expensive portrait houses in the nearest large city. Not to mention another three or so local shooters who also charge large amounts.

Unless you are friends with the executive, and then, only with care if you are not sufficiently intimate to be considered a possible candidate for godfathering one of his children, comment only on the female through conversation about the picture itself.

"What a lovely photograph" is a common line. If the executive wants to get more personal, his response will be "My wife." That's the cue for an even more intimate remark: "Beautiful lady." Never say, "You're a lucky man," as this implies good fortune dictated his attaining the hand of the woman, instead of his own worth, wealth, and sexiness. A safer, less personal response to the "my wife" line would be, if you recognize the shutter snapper's logo, "I see that Rudolpho (or other name) took it. An excellent choice. His work is so . . ." The " . . ." could be words like "exacting," "realistic," or "dramatic." Descriptions such as "angelic," "beautiful," or "haunting" will be taken as a reference to the woman again, and start the conversation onto the same merry-go-round.

VASTLANDers carry family shots in their wallets or purses. Picture portability is important because so much time is spent outside the office. If anyone here waited for business to come to him/her, he/she would be old and gray before it happened. You want something, you go where it is, and discuss it with folks who have it.

Personal effects in the VASTLANDS office, then, aside from guns and an occasional display of mounted animal heads stuffed as trophies, are not numerous. A rack of pipes is nice, but as the smokeless society grows, it has less cachet. When resistance to smoking gains enough force to pass laws affecting behavior in private offices, the pipe, at least in the VASTLANDS among business executives, will regain lost glory. It will be another way of saying, "I do as I damn well please."

Personal belongings belong at home or in the truck. Not in the business place. It's a regional belief.

WONDERLAND executives are enthusiastic over photographs. Especially color or black-and-white, eight-by-ten glossies. No comment is expected or required, as they are placed on display as a statement.

Typical shots include the executive playing golf, fishing, or otherwise cavorting with actors/actresses from the stage, silver screen, and television. Most valuable of these is the executive and one star, smiling at each other, shaking hands, having dinner, etc. Naturally, the autograph will read, "For my dearest old buddy," or some line demonstrating intimacy.

Similar groupings with politicians, including the president of the U.S., are also acceptable, but a little more sensitive. In the case of a presidential picture, with original handwriting thanking the executive for some form of national service, or recognizing that person's contribution to anything but the president's campaign fund, the ground is pretty safe. A visiting client or boss will be impressed and not take umbrage even if they are of a different political persuasion or hate some presidential actions. Best to stop there, though, as the same spirit does not extend to the secretary of state, a senator, or the vice president. Photographs of congressional members are virtually worthless, except as fill-ins, because no one has any idea who they are and it is indecent for the executive to have to explain.

There is a well-established rule about the hanging of celebrity testimonial (celeb-test) shots. The only time one, and only one, photo may be displayed is when it is of the president. Even then, the exhibitor had better have others on which to fall back. Aside from presidential pix, the executive needs a second display of at least five, and better still, ten celeb-test pix. Or the impression will be negative. Instead of appearing to know many, many celebrities, the executive appears to be depending upon a single acquaintance.

Another trend, also along the lines of the celeb-test photo display, appears to be spreading from WONDERLAND toward the East. Power Accessorizing is the use of personally-owned symbols to demonstrate personal importance. Many of these items can be rented in WONDERLAND because there are numerous firms catering to the TV/film production needs of accessorizing sets.

Examples of Power Accessories, and typical comments made by the executive when a visitor takes notice of a particular piece, are as follows:

Item	*Comment*
Fragment of moon rock embedded in plastic	"Buzz sent me that. Said he thought about blasting off in a rocket built by the lowest bidder and wished I'd been there."
Vial of crude oil mounted on an old sedimentary rock with a brass plate reading "North Sea Oil"	"Ever see crude? Looks like mud. Margaret sent that to me."
Three 35mm film frames in a silver and glass press	"The last scene Gary ever filmed. His wife wanted me to have it."
Single Indian feather, tufted and wrapped with bead-work at the base	"Only feather in the world worth ten grand. Hell, Scouts are a good cause, so I kicked in."

Power Accessories are an improvement over celeb-test pix because manners dictate some comment from the executive when guests discover the object. Their puzzled expressions demand response, thus allowing the perfect name drop or self-aggrandizing statement. This nefarious technique is spreading quite rapidly. Look for it in your neighborhood soon.

Photographs of family are also popular in HEARTLAND, but show subtle differences. Black-and-white, and smaller than those gracing desks even in NATURELAND, there is a pre-1960 flavor to the dress, poses, and look of the men, women, and children.

Farm scenes, for some odd reason, are favored by farmer-executives who, one would think, get to see quite enough of farms in real life. There is no accounting for tastes because a beloved cow or pig may also be an image frozen for posterity.

At least part of HEARTLAND, as well as a segment of VASTLANDS and MEXICA, is so smitten by the cowboy mystique as to display various makes of barbed wire. Foot-long lengths are mounted on shellacked boards. Names of the original designers or manufacturers and the dates and places of use are burned into soft wood. The appearance is supposed to be rustic-western, but is closer to a Cub Scout camp gift for dad. These plaques are in copious display at collector gatherings, where a single strand of some weird but scarce wire sells for several thousand dollars. When displayed in an office, these wire boards are usually accompanied by other strange and wonderful accoutrements, the most favored of which is a chair made completely of horns from longhorn cattle with a tufted, red leather seat. If you've never seen such a thing, it's your loss.

One last trend, now so common in INDUSTRIA as to draw no notice whatsoever, is the modular office. Every bankrupt fiberglass boat builder in the United States, searching for an even simpler way to apply their limited technology, first turned trailer and motorhome manufacturer. When this fad fell flatter than the down-to-the-sea-in-ships craze, there was a sigh of relief throughout the industry. Those mobile homes were hard to build. Portable dividers, used as fake walls from which designers could hang a work surface and shelves, were just appearing in decorator and interior designer trade magazines. No great skill was needed to make a four-by-seven-foot rectangle and cover it with vinyl or fabric in solid color or pattern. The modular offices system was on its way.

Today, huge catalogues show brand after brand of portable partitions and endless lists of accessories all planned to interlock, uninterlock, and reinterlock in a new way.

The modular office, at best, gives a level of privacy just short of the exercise yard in a state prison immediately after lunch break.

Executives charged with operations first embraced the dividers as a means of housing more people in less space while giving the image of private quarters. They quickly found that the system demanded more room than normal if any level of privacy was to be maintained. Sound carried, regardless of the number of special ceiling tiles and hanging baffles designed to muffle it.

Modular office space can be nice. Especially when the alternative is the open bullpen. It is gaining acceptance, and more and more operations in INDUSTRIA, especially those in big metro areas, are using it as a means of offsetting escalating costs of interior finish work and remaining flexible. You undoubtedly have seen one system or another. You may even be housed in it. If so, thank the frenetic minds of INDUSTRIA for making it possible. This is one trend that didn't begin in WONDERLAND.

As shown, regional differences occur in office size, decor, and use of personal accessories. With this information, keen observation on your part will allow you to detect the executive who has crossed the line, moving from one zone to another.

CHAPTER

7

TELEPHONE TACTICS

Understanding what was meant
by what wasn't said

Business use of the telephone varies in different regions of
the U.S. by a surprising degree. Since one of the most common contacts executives have with peers from other zones
occurs by telephone, defining the point at which one's use
becomes another's abuse, and vice versa, is important.

The original Bell patent in March, 1876, was quickly put
to commercial use. Initial installations were direct. One instrument was straight-wired to another. The concept of having all lines run to a central switchboard, which had the capability to join any pair of speaker-receivers, followed quickly.

First connections were in the COMMERCIAL CORRI-
DOR and spread into the CONSERVATORY and INDUS-
TRIA. Development was done state by state, then groups of
states were linked, and, finally, the groups joined into a nationwide telephone system.

The arrival of telephone service in a new area was a major event. Those in the South, for instance, heard about the
electronic wonder long before it was available, and envied
their northern cousins in New York City for a further demonstration of sophistication and urbanity.

Regionally, use of the telephone acquired different emotional connotations. Those who waited did so reverently, and used the instrument more sparingly than those to whom access was normal.

Such diverse views also affected the type, length, and formality of conversation deemed suitable by telephone. It is this cluster of traditions, carried through to the present, that influences various regions' concepts of "correct" telephone usage.

CONSERVATORY:

Frugality is a virtue in the CONSERVATORY, so it is only natural the telephone should be used frugally. Economies extend to length of conversation as well as number of calls.

When talking to business executives in this zone, don't call unless it's important, keep preamble amenities to a minimum, get to the point quickly, and hang up before you overstay your welcome. If you are called by someone in the CONSERVATORY, display a prudent attitude. Assume they called to tell you something or ask a question. Listen to what they say without superfluous comment and answer questions succinctly. Then hang up. If you are asked only one question, you will know the answer is vital to the caller. Why? Because in the CONSERVATORY, common practice would be to accumulate questions as they arise, and unless one is of overriding importance, call once and ask all.

The same inclination against wasting telephone calls is aided and abetted by another traditionalist attitude. The U.S. Government runs one of the most reliable, if not swiftest, postal services on earth. If anyone in the CONSERVATORY wishes to communicate on a subject of importance, he or she will write a letter. This is a key to comprehending the CONSERVATORY business attitude. If it's important, please be sufficiently genteel as to write. Besides, a stamp is far less costly than a long distance call.

No matter how hard you try, you will not be able to outdo the CONSERVATORY executive's brevity. Do not mistake it as impoliteness. It is bred in the bone.

COMMERCIAL CORRIDOR:

Business telephone conversations here take a consistent, explicit pattern. Follow it and you'll be rewarded. Deviate and you will be perceived as an oddball executive.

COMMERCIAL CORRIDOR Telephone Conversation Pattern:

Speech	Commentary
"Hello, John. Robert here." (Also "Hi" is used.)	Spoken with enthusiasm. Use of first names mandatory, even with strangers. Opening words are spoken as if you just met on the street and were pumping the person's hand energetically.
(Following whatever answer John makes, no matter how unenthusiastic) "Great! How's the weather down (or out) there?"	Meteorological preoccupation is endemic in the CORRIDOR. Business people seem weather obsessive. This subject is used as an opening question even when a Manhattanite calls Pittsburgh in the middle of a January blizzard. Caller's enthusiasm does not wane in the slightest.
(Following, no matter what answer is made to the weather question.) "Great! Snowing here, too. Really cold."	Even more enthusiasm, if at all possible, in an effort to make the callee feel the caller is really enjoying the conversation. No mat-

ter what response to the weather query, the caller never one-ups. In fact, the caller one-downs. If it's bright, mild, and sunny (i.e., a perfect day in the callee's town), the CORRIDOR caller will report snow, freezing rain, a 30-knot wind, and temperatures in the low teens. In other words, he or she will place the worst face on the weather possible. This is a ploy intended to gain empathy, if not outright sympathy. And in the case of New Yorkers, give the callee an outlet for releasing envy the caller knows is generated in the country cousin by his or her more polished presence.

(There is no break with the above speech. Read this as "Great! Snowing here, too. Really cold.")

"Say, John?"

(Also without pause for response) "About that report on the Mixupper-doppler. I thought that was supposed to be on my desk this morning."

or

"I thought that was due today."

The question is spoken casually, voice still enthusiastic. This signifies end of amenities and start of business.

Superior calling inferior.

or

Equal calling equal. (If there is any doubt about superiority in the executive hierarchy, the equal mode will be used while the COMMERCIAL CORRIDOR executive works to gain superiority.)

                              or

". . . is about due, and I'm already getting calls from (first name of superior to both individuals) about it."

Inferior calling superior and invoking the name of someone superior to both caller and callee, in an effort to level the disparity of their positions.

This discussion could continue for several minutes, with the caller chastising the inferior callee, cajoling his or her equal, or attempting to find a way to get the desired information without incurring the wrath of a superior. Once this process is concluded, it's time for the sign-off.

"Well, got to go. Got a meeting. I'm running it and can't be late. I'll get back to you. Thanks."

Return to robust enthusiasm. The style is more important than what is said, except closing lines must be brief to suggest, without saying so, that the caller has an enormous work load and must immediately switch attention to other pressing matters.

Ideally, the enthusiasm should also carry a complex message, combining equal parts of don't-pity-me, I'm-strong-and-can-take-all-this-load, and where-would-this-organization-be-without-me.

That's a tall order, but many CORRIDOR callers can do it, and at the same time imply the work load of the person being called is not so great as theirs. Also present is a man-to-man (man-to-woman, woman-to-woman) element suggesting that although the reason for the call was business, the two of you are really humanists and deal with each other accordingly.

A properly schooled CORRIDOR caller in full stride on a good day is a formidable telephonist. Opening and closing ploys will not vary but, with each use, will become more effective. CORRIDOR callers, overall, view the telephone as an instrument designed to allow the caller to communicate on many levels at the same time. The only defense when dealing with a CORRIDOR caller (if you are not one yourself) is to allow the emotional nuance to roll over you and counter with subtleties of your own. Good luck. Years of experience and practice went into learning COMMERCIAL CORRIDOR telephone skills.

SOUTHLANDS:

"Well, shut ma mouf."

That phrase spells out the attitude of the true southern business executive from any of the three regions. Raised in a telephone tradition which holds that long distance calls are costly and any news someone phones long distance to relate is not news you want to hear, executives in this area approach the telephone with trepidation. Mingled, perhaps, with a dollop of distaste.

Atlanta, with its foreign (read out-of-state) influences, dampens this attitude, but the Old Guard here carries more than a residual negative bias.

Outside Atlanta, excepting New Orleans, which is excepted from almost everything, long distance telephoning is not used with impunity. Careful records are maintained so every call can be accounted for and, where proper agreements exist, charged to the appropriate account.

Other than teenagers, no one in the South, and that includes the business community, feels emotionally secure on the telephone. This leads to a lessening of use and shorter conversations.

That outlook, combined with relative ease in moving one's body from here to there, makes face-to-face meetings more common than in the COMMERCIAL CORRIDOR or the CONSERVATORY. Face-to-face meetings are more satisfactory to a Southerner, as there are more opportunities for pre- and post-business amenities. And amenities in the SOUTHLANDS are appreciated.

Telephone calls, then, are reserved for rather rapid exchanges of information and, occasionally, opinion on very important or very unimportant subjects. Important ones call for contact that cannot wait for a personal meeting, and unimportant ones need to be handled, but are minor enough to be dealt with without meeting. Midrange problems are the best for face-to-face discussion, so are reserved for that purpose. These are matters serious enough to hold interest, yet not likely to lead to confrontation.

In the SOUTHLANDS, business executives are somewhat loath to return a call. This stems from the knowledge, based on practical experience, that the chances of receiving good news upon recall are about equal to winning the Croatian National Lottery. And then getting paid. If it's good news, the caller will try and try again, because it's fun to be the bearer of good tidings. At best, returning a call will net a request for funds, under the guise of a civic endeavor, or, at worst, will provide perfectly awful information any sane person could have done without.

Calling into the South, unless you are from the SOUTH-LANDS, you may need an interpreter. Slower speech patterns, accent, and multi-syllable pronunciation of one-syllable words are not compatible with the resonant capabilities of even an ultramodern telephone, which is probably another reason the area hesitates to use the device.

INDUSTRIA:

Concise and precise, without inhibitions.

That's the telephone pattern of manufacturing America. Tell it like it is, cut the baloney, get it over with, and don't be afraid to show emotion. Especially anger. The most mild-mannered managers in this region become rabid, roaring tigers over the telephone when they believe there is reason or cause for indignation. They say things they would never say to a person face-to-face.

INDUSTRIA call tradition mandates efficiency. One gets to the point as directly as possible, has the needed amount of conversation, and terminates the exchange.

Amenities such as pre/post-discussion of weather, sports, or headlines, except among those personally acquainted and who enjoy some form of relationship outside the office, are rare. This is much more the "John, Roger here. Gumspaw Mechanics. Say. What about the twelve blue-terror wiggims we ordered?"

Please remember when calling into this area, no one intends to be rude. In fact, they would be surprised if taken that way. Get them on the phone, get it said, and get off the line. That's the way phone calls should be handled.

HEARTLAND AMERICA:

Never, ever say what you've called to say until you are current on the state of the family, including relatives, business activities, and all upcoming social events anticipated by the callee. Do not expect the callee to respond to your inquiries or react to your news until he or she is completely in possession of like information from you.

In sodbuster days, families lived far, far apart. Get-togethers became talk-fests. Men went off in a group and ladies formed a separate cluster. Partially, this was to prevent a couple from having to waste valuable time around people speaking to each other. They had enough of that day in and day out, without interruption, to last a lifetime, or make a short time seem like a lifetime. Not that our pioneer forefathers and foremothers didn't have a variety of exciting topics for discussion. Both worked, as they say in the HEARTLAND, from "too early to until too late to"—before sunup until after sundown. By the time work was done for the day, they were too. Done in, that is. What talking they did centered on what they had to do to eke out another day's living from the land.

This lifestyle continued into the 1900s with little change. Then the arrival of electricity made life easier almost overnight. Widespread use of the telephone was not far behind.

First received as an almost mystical gift, telephones soon became the center of community social life. On the old party-line system, where each family was supposed to answer only a set sequence of rings (e.g.: one long; or three short; or one long, one short), the number of people who would "listen in" was, at times, troublesome. As each person picked up a receiver, electrical energy carrying the signal was bled off. On a four party line, with three phones already off the hook before the person for whom the call was intended answered, the voice on the other end was mighty weak. This usually resulted in one party-line member chiding the others to "hang off this line so I can hear" (or words to that effect).

At times, eavesdroppers could become overwrought with the drama revealed in another's life and, forgetting themselves, would gasp aloud or suddenly blurt advice, in much the same way ardent TV soap opera fans do today. Instead, however, of talking to an inanimate TV, their observations were heard by two people actually living the situation. The telephone in HEARTLAND was pure, simple, down-home fun, and is still treated that way.

This is how the regional attitude toward business telephone conversations came to be. By understanding it, you will be able to slip into the correct mode when necessary.

As a rule, there are no strangers over the phone. A businessman calls another whom he has not met. He wants an appointment to discuss a money matter. The conversation will start with general "howdies," an exchange of names, and might proceed to a discussion of potential relationships ("You say you're a Butterworth? There's a Butterworth over to Chukatee. Right good stock man. He your kin?"). Talk is certain to include the latest on each person's family health, the state of the agribusiness, the generally deplorable condition of our nation, the growing looseness of kids' morals, and a leisurely review of how slipshod American products have become. This process can be as short as ten minutes, if both parties are in a hurry, or as long as a half hour, if both have time. (Actually, it only takes one with sufficient time. The other sincerely enjoys the conversation and would never be rude to someone over the telephone anyway.)

The business portion follows. If they have attained a meeting of minds on other topics, find mutual ground through acquaintanceship with family relations, or just think there might be a good argument in it, they agree to meet. This empathy test is usually administered in two or, at the most, three questions. Then, without an awkward silence, work done, they segue back into conversation. ("Ya say you're old Butterworth's second cousin on his mother's side, twice removed, huh? Well, I'll be. Sure is a small world.") It continues for another few minutes before one or the other's "Well, be seein' ya." The close is always a "Thanks for callin'," said sincerely, because the callee is always glad to use the phone, even for a wrong number.

Wrong numbers among business executives calling into

the area can be enjoyable. Several have reported lengthy conversations with people reached by mistake. Talk centers on helping the caller find the correct party, a process which involves reminiscences, discussions of possible candidates and, in one case, an invitation to supper, "next time you're down this way."

Confidential matters, due at least in part to the old party-line tradition that lingered here into the post-World War II years, are seldom discussed by telephone. Not even in a vague or coded fashion. The meaning might be kept from a potential listener, but the mere fact the two individuals have a confidence between them is not seemly. Private business stays that way. Private. And "There ain't nothin' private about telephone talk."

If you are from another zone and place a business call into HEARTLAND, settle back and relax. It might take a while, but you'll get a lot more done by going with the flow than contesting every inch, showing bad manners, if not poor taste, by making grudging answers or being uncommunicative.

VASTLANDS:

The telephone is a vital business tool in the VASTLANDS. Portable receivers, briefcase units, car phones, headsets in aircraft, and at least two or three instruments in every home show their necessity. Telephones in all styles and of many capabilities abound.

Auto units are popular because the amount of driving leaves ample time for returning calls, an act done with nearly religious fervor. Business people also do not limit telephone use to business hours. The rule is call anyone anytime anywhere. The callee will be happy to receive the contact.

Distance driving, as a way of life, also imposes limitations. The only store which sells refills for the company's imported gas chromatograph analyzer is in Blue Canyon. Before driving forty miles there, then forty back, a single call makes sense. The shop may be out of stock on the item. It may be out of business completely. (Businesses not only come and go in the VASTLANDS, they alter their main lines of activity to accommodate changing conditions. What is stocked today, because of a new mining operation, can be unstocked tomorrow.)

Telephone calls are punctuated with what has come to be known as the Vast Silence.

Example:

"Hey, Jim? Pete."	Pete calls Jim. First name always.
"Hey, Pete."	Tone shows Jim recognizes Pete.
"How you?"	Direct inquiry from Pete to Jim.
	Pause of ten seconds. Ten seconds does not seem a long period. Time it while holding a telephone in your hand, waiting for the other party to respond
"Pretty fair."	Another, shorter pause. Four seconds.
"You?"	Jim returns the inquiry.
"Oh, 'bout the same."	Spoken after only a few polite seconds wait.

Scintillating banter continues for what seems to be an interminable period. After discovering both are in approximately the same state of health as when they parted twelve hours earlier after four beers at Karl's Kliffside Kanteen, where they almost came to agreement on an oil lease, the two carry on, not with discussion of their business, but with other inanities relating to weather. (VASTLANDers are not as weather obsessive as those in the COMMERCIAL CORRIDOR. Weather in the VASTLANDS can be of life or death importance. If a pass is snowed closed, or a storm is already dropping ice in one area but has not yet moved into another, advance warning can be valuable.) VASTLANDers also silence their way through the subjects of fishing or new ski boots.

The art of Vast Silences is learned. It is not enough to simply shut your mouth and maintain muteness. Your thoughts must be true. Picture a forest ranger gazing over the green, treed expanse of a mountain. An eagle soars. See this in your head. Appreciate it. Then respond. The way you say your next line will be markedly affected by this vision.

Do not be deceived into thinking you can keep your mouth shut, time yourself by your gold wristwatch, and every ten seconds or so say something appropriate. The tone of your voice will give you away every time. There has to be that wistful, soulful sound, or the other party will know you are an imposter.

Another VASTLANDS trait, when speaking with a business compatriot over the phone, is always to make it appear as if the two have not seen or talked together for at least a week. It helps both parties preserve the feeling of isolation and vastness of the region.

NATURELAND:

The Primary Precept is easy: The telephone is déclassé. Unsightly wires are strung in vista-disturbing lines across pristine countryside. Until receivers became available, with strident bell replaced by electronic turkey warbles, the instruments themselves were distasteful. The new sound is more acceptable, but the stigma has not worn away.

At times, déclassé or no, one must use the telephone. There is simply no other way. Thus, Precept Two: State your business as quickly as possible. Do not dawdle. Your call has intruded on the privacy of another. Even if the other trusts you and knows you would not call unless it was absolutely necessary, the less said, the better. As opposed to broaching a subject over the telephone, which might take some time to discuss, use the call to make an appointment to meet. This is considered preferable to a long telephone tête-à-tête. No matter that in order to meet it is necessary to drive fifty miles of foggy mountain road. Each drive through NATURELAND is a privilege, not an inconvenience.

Precept Two, then, may be restated as follows: The best way to keep your call short is to use it to make an appointment to discuss, in person, what you needed to call for in the first place. In practice, this is even more complex than it sounds.

One other NATURELAND curiosity. Understanding the previous paragraphs should make it obvious that the COMMERCIAL CORRIDOR's darling, call-forwarding, is a no-no here. And the pager, a device dear to the heart of executives in other regions, is a devil's machine which connects straight to hell. How else could one view a contraption which hunts you down in unlikely places and urges your attention by disturbing those around you?

WONDERLAND:

The telephone. Joy of life in WONDERLAND! The most revered modern convenience next to the automobile. With it, an executive can call next door or around the world. Think how many more people that makes accessible to each and every sales pitch.

In WONDERLAND, the telephone is not a communications instrument. It is a device by which the caller can dominate the person being called. To what end? You name it. Anything from information to a demand for money.

Keep this principle in mind when using the phone in WONDERLAND: Anyone you call will instantly know you

want something from them. Or want them to do something.
So they are on guard from the first warble or bell. This fact
helps explain the rather strange pattern business telephone
conversations assume in WONDERLAND.

The first phase of a call is the laying on of terms of en-
dearment. "Bunky, baby, lover," and the endless use of
mawkish diminutives ("Bootsie, sweetie," or "Annette, cu-
tey, lovey") are a clear giveaway the caller is engaging in the
WONDERLAND Syndrome.

Lavish praise follows endearments. ("I heard you did the
Buchouse Deal! Bunky, that's great. Only a man of your lim-
itless imagination and creativity could have seen a way to
make it work. You're the greatest, Bunky, baby. Tops. The
ab-so-lute highest.")

The praise may be sincere. A well-done job is as admired
by peers in WONDERLAND as elsewhere, although the ef-
fluent expressions used to show that admiration may be a bit
baroque. One excellent test to reveal sincerity lies in the
specific nature of the praise. If it is for a successful activity,
fine; directed toward a general trait, probably not. "Your mind,
Janie, sweetest! The sharpest" is a comment aimed at a general trait.

Lavish praise is followed by the purpose of the call, usually stated in reverse. This twist is difficult to explain, but
may be seen in the following demonstrative dialogue:

"Look, sweetie, I'm going to do you a hell of a favor. Your ol' Uncle Jim is coming through for you." (without pause for any speech by the person being rewarded.)	Jim Norton, the caller, wants to do a real estate deal.
"Know that house you've got up near the Canyon? The one you wanted to rent?	The person being called does have a house near a canyon, but has no interest in renting it

"I've got the deal of a life-time. Not to rent it. That's a mistake, by the way. What's that? You never intended to rent it? Smart. You are so smart. Of course you shouldn't rent it. Didn't I just agree and say it was a mistake to rent it?"
(without pause)
"Like I say, you should sell it. And I've got a buyer who is willing to pay the price."

A reverse sell, in an effort to come to some agreement with the home owner.

The reason for the call is now clear to both caller and callee. The "reverse" is completed. The caller contacts the home owner in hopes of making a deal, but reverses the situation so it appears he is acting at that individual's behest while, at the same time, doing the person a favor.

Does this technique work? On the surface, it wouldn't seem to. Especially in a zone where everyone is practicing it. But proof of efficacy is often seen in consistent, long-term use of a practice. This one has been around for a half century.

Someone highly skilled in the technique, possessed of a sufficiently thick skin so as to ignore pointed barbs, and driven by a need to dominate others can be effective.

From this discourse, it should be clear that, as stated, the primary use of the telephone in WONDERLAND is for the caller to control the person called. Anyone receiving a phone call should automatically be forewarned and prepared to forfend the caller.

With this as an underlying premise, what motivation is there for anyone to return a telephone call? There is none at all. So, contrary to promises of receptionist or secretary, leaving a number is a waste of time. A return call will occur only when the person called wants something from the caller. Badly enough to brave the caller's attempt to get what he/she wants.

It's a rather tough system, but everyone knows where he/she stands, all the time.

MEXICA:

MEXICA is the land of the unintelligible telephone response. On the presumption that nothing you say can be used against you unless someone else can understand it, business telephone conversations in MEXICA are exemplary examples of evasiveness. It is a matter of pride that nothing is ever decided over the phone. Nothing anyone can hold you to, at least.

Example: "Look. Do you want this deal or don't you?"
"Of course."
"Good. Then let's get together and settle the details."
"Fine. Got to go now. Big meeting. Talk to you soon."

The above is an example of an actual conversation between a COMMERCIAL CORRIDOR executive who had been trying for three weeks to get a yes or no answer from a MEXICA businesswoman. Evasiveness is not based on gender. It's a regional trait. Go over the words. It's all positive, but no information is offered. "Of course" is not "yes." It is also not "no." It is neither. And no appointment was set for future negotiation. In reality, the MEXICA executive was eager to enter into the agreement. She was simply approached wrong.

Howard Hughes, the reclusive, eccentric multi-billionaire, was born and raised in MEXICA. He left to continue his business career in WONDERLAND, but he took with him one of MEXICA's strongest traits; to wit:

Never close a deal or hire a person until the last nanosecond before the absolute ultimate deadline to do so.

The reason for this quaint trait is based on an obvious truth:

Something may happen before the final moment the deal is consummated to change your mind.

Delay and evasion, then, have become the basis for much telephone talk in MEXICA.

MEXICA phone amenities are as long or short as the caller wishes to make them. Note that the caller is in charge. The person being called will respond in kind, following the caller's lead, until the latter feels it is time to talk business.

Instead of "Look, do you want to do this deal or don't you?"—a sentence with a certain crudeness, perhaps even a veiled threat—there is a more gracious approach:

"Our time has almost run out. Do you wish to act?"

"Of course."

"I have to say yes or no for you by six this evening."

"I can't have an answer for you by then."

"I'll try and get 'til nine in the morning."

"You do that."

"Okay. But if I can't I'll have to put you down as a no. Unless I hear from you before six. This evening."

The above is a much improved style and would be admired in MEXICA. The decision maker is given a deadline and told what will happen if there is no response. The caller also has left the door open for further talk. If there is no response and the caller wishes to continue the matter, he or she simply waits until the next day, then announces success in gaining requested extra time. This in itself is a method of ferreting out actual interest of the other party. If he/she is happy with the extension, he/she will let the caller know. If not, that will be made clear, too.

The exception to this rule is found in the oil patch, which operates in exception to many American business rules.

Oil patch executives pride themselves on making a decision, making it fast, and sticking to it. This has to do with the traditions of drilling for oil, where actions costing thousands have to be ordered from the floor of the rig, *now*.

Oil fielders subscribe to the Howard Hughes House Rules of Procrastination, but hide it better than most. They also do much of their business over the phone, so if you want instruction on how to overcome vaguenesses in the MEXICA business culture, you won't find better teachers.

No telephone device has caused greater problems here than the call-holding "click" warning. It is best in MEXICA not to install this device into your phone system. You will thus be saved an inordinate amount of grief and tension.

Example: You have a caller on the line. Your conversation is important, but not vital. What is vital is the call you are longing to receive—a go-ahead for a special project from your company president.

The line clicks, notifying you another party has dialed your number. It could be your president with good news.

The dilemma: Under Macho Morality of MEXICA, if you ask your caller to hold while you check the incoming call, you will grievously offend him/her. After all, they were on the line with you before some Johnny-come-lately upstart signaled for your attention. And what if you were the one who placed the call? Under the code of Macho, you *owe* it to the person with whom you are speaking to complete your conversation in a leisurely, relaxed manner.

You can be sure if you heard the line "click," they did, too, and are waiting to see how you handle it. Even if you had time to explain your predicament, offense would still be taken if you leave him/her on hold to follow up on the other caller.

There are some things it is better not to know. Second caller on line is one. At least in MEXICA.

WASHINGTON, D.C.:

In a land where no one listens and everyone speaks, the telephone is not a useful instrument. In spite of this, the city has 179 telephones per hundred residents. More than any other place on earth! Even so, in Washington, it is improbable, if not impossible, for anyone to receive any information concerning anything he/she might wish to know through the medium of a telephone call.

Less than industrious receptionists and secretaries use the telephone to arrange their personal lives, set their luncheon dates, and check on their children. They do not use the telephone to provide information to a caller. To prevent this from inadvertently happening, they have developed a high standard of contumelious evasion. There are notable exceptions to this rule, and when you discover one, praise him or her highly. Write thank you letters to his/her boss, for inclusion into the personnel records, and assign that name a slot in your phone file. Here is a treasured resource.

Most often, though, and it makes no difference if you are calling locally or long distance, you get to play Referral Roundup. In this fascinating telephone tag game, you seek a certain individual or specific information, and others conspire against you. The contest begins when you dial a number. Play starts with the first ring. If there is any way to do it without appearing negligent, the assigned answerer will allow the telephone to ring at least five or six times before responding.

When the receptionist comes on the line, you may say anything you like, as it will make no difference whatsoever. The game, also played in more limited forms through the halls of large corporations in the COMMERCIAL CORRIDOR and INDUSTRIA, is afoot.

In a federal office, unlike a business, where if a client receives this type of treatment, management will hear about it, there is no recourse to authority. So the game lasts as long as your patience, or long distance budget, holds out.

In play, receptionist "A" refers you to secretary or assistant "B," who in turn refers you to "C," then "D," "E," "F," "G," and so on. Order varies. The goal is to take the longest possible time to keep you in hope of eventually completing your call. Success is judged in two ways. First, by the number of different people who come on the line to speak with you before your disgust forces you to hang up. Second, by the total length of time the aggregate group keeps you on hold while they "look up a number" or other such balderdash.

Skilled players can string an inexperienced executive along well over an hour. No published records are maintained, but times in the forty-minute range are commonly spoken of in the halls.

It is a painful truth that if you ever manage to contact the person to whom you wished to speak, you are likely to be disappointed. Why? Because of the first comment made in this section. A telephone is not much use to one who talks but never listens. And it's not much use for you to listen, and listen, and listen without ever being able to ask your questions or get a straight response.

Other Washington, D.C. telephone contests include determining how long someone will stay on hold without hanging up; how, when that same person calls back, to act innocent; and how many times an operator can cut off a caller before the caller goes mad and stops trying.

Large corporations all have variations of these and other phone sports, but none has raised the standard of play as high as those jolly jesters in the Capital.

MIAMI:

Effective phone use can be hard in this town. Especially if you do not speak Spanish. All the forces discussed as working in MEXICA are laboring here, too. Many with a vengeance. Add a widespread phobia of telephone tapping, a common area practice, and it is quite difficult to discuss anything of a confidential nature with any confidence at all.

One telephone peccadillo found in smaller communities can be summed up by a rule first promulgated by H.L. Mencken, the Baltimore newspaper writer-philosopher of the 1920s. To paraphrase Mencken, mail left unanswered for a period of six weeks answers itself. In other words, if the message is important, whoever is trying to reach you will try again.

According to small town philosophy, if it's a call from someone outside the city limits, do not call back. In all probability, you'll only end up spending your good money to hear an appeal you could well do without. At least let the caller ring on his or her own nickel (or dollar).

A fine point of etiquette lies in the use of first names. If the person you are calling is superior to you in your organization, or in your general area of business, do you start by using his/her first name? What if the person is of the opposite sex? What about a prospect you are contacting for the first time? What about someone older than you who occupies a position in your company inferior to yours? These are all knotty quandaries with regional variations in what is considered to be proper.

The CONSERVATORY, after a close race by the SOUTHLANDS, is the nation's winner in the formality derby. Formal behavior here is always correct. Unless the person to whom you are speaking is (A) younger and you have known him/her since childhood, or (B) in your family, use the appropriate Mr., Mrs., Miss, or Ms., and stick to last names. Anyone calling into the CONSERVATORY on a business matter from any other area of the United States has no problem at all. Be formal and you'll be right. Be casual and you'll be undone.

The basic phone ploy of the COMMERCIAL CORRIDOR demands use of first name because it sounds idiotic to be blatantly enthusiastic while addressing someone as Mr., Mrs., Miss, or Ms. The words and speech pattern are mutually incompatible. So if you use the COMMERCIAL CORRIDOR approach, use first names from the opening word after "Hi" or "Hello."

Calling from outside, be last name formal or first name

casual. It doesn't matter, as everyone in the CORRIDOR uses only first names in conversation.

Formality is the best rule in the SOUTHLANDS, especially if you are not a Southerner. Use of the word "sir" to those older, regardless of position in the company hierarchy, is also approved.

Pay particular attention to the use of Mrs. or Miss, and avoid the Ms. ("Miz") form of address. Southern accents confuse this somewhat, because "Mrs." ("Misses" in the rest of America) is pronounced "Miz" in the SOUTHLANDS anyway. So if you say "Miz" (Ms.) over the phone, the female on the other end, accustomed to local pronunciation, will think you believe her to be married. Married businesswomen in the SOUTHLANDS will correct you if you say "Miss." Their response will be an automatic "Miz." The declaration won't be in a tone of rebuke, but it probably will be mentioned. Calling an unwed female "Miz" will probably bring a gentle, correcting, "Uh, Miss. I'm a Miss."

Manners in INDUSTRIA are not so formalized. If your contact seems to be going rather well after the first minute or so, throw in a first name. If your first name use passes unnoticed, switch back and forth. If the respondent uses your first name, stay on that basis. If there is resistance, return to more formal address.

In other areas, except MEXICA, go to first name as soon as identities have been exchanged.

Example: Bob Jackson calls Tom Bryan. "Mr. Bryan, Bob Jackson here. Hope everything's going well today."

"Well as can be expected, Bob."

"Tom, I wonder if . . ."

Nine times in ten, the callee will quickly start first name use, if you give him or her the opportunity.

Do watch for one thing, though. In these regions, care is needed when members of the opposite gender speak on the telephone. If you have been introduced or talked at least twice before, then fire off first names right away.

"Jennifer? Bill Thorpe."

"Hi, Bill."

That exchange is perfect.

If this is the first contact between opposite sexes, be more circumspect.

"Mrs. Blaffer? Bill Thorpe."

"Hello, Bill."

"Jennifer, have you seen . . ."

If the female executive responds with the male's first name, then both should use first names. If she does not, the male should remain formal.

In MEXICA and Miami, informality among men is fine, as long as rigid formality with women is maintained. Ladies expect it. Secretaries can be won by using a single "Miss" in a conversation. This is not to imply that after the use of the first "Miss" you switch to a first name. The fact is that male callers are likely not to use any name at all. "Little lady, is Bob Jackson in?" is an opening-sentence case in point.

Another thought. Please notice that when discussing younger secretaries, the gender word is automatically "Miss." This is because there are no younger male secretaries. It's part of the territorial tradition. And married women who work as secretaries are accustomed to being called "Miss."

In Washington, D.C., be formal at all costs, with everyone. Best friends, perhaps, excepted. Staying formal will help carry you through the rigors of Phone Games.

Be especially formal with women, and do not be afraid to ask if the proper title is "Miss" or "Mrs." She will tell you if "Ms." is appropriate.

Do not get first name cozy over the telephone in Washington during business calls. In the long run, this will cause more grief than you can believe. Washington is a "favor" town, and by assuming an intimate mode of address, you leave yourself open for endless requests for favors from people you hardly know, who are certainly unable to repay your service in kind. Granting favors in Washington is tricky. Do not make it worse by hanging an open invitation in public. Stay formal for all business conducted by telephone. You won't regret it.

Let's close this commentary on telephone manners and mannerisms with a few short paragraphs on the subject of listening. Research reveals one simple fact that will make every executive a more effective telephone communicator. Overwhelmingly, the largest single class of complaints on various aspects of communications focuses on listening.

Emphasis in schools and colleges has been placed on speaking and writing effectively. But listening is the other part of the communications process.

A few short paragraphs on this subject were promised. Here they are.

When talking to a business colleague or prospect on the phone, listen.

Let the other person express his/her complete thought. Don't interrupt in mid-sentence.

Listen. To what others say, and the tone they use to say it. Voice can often reveal as much as words.

Listen. To what you are saying. It may not be what you want to say.

Listen.

As soon as the other person stops speaking, do not jump right in. Think about what was said. Then respond.

Listen. Then speak. Then listen again.

You'll improve your work efficiency, your prospects in your organization, and your relationships with clients. Just by listening instead of concentrating on what you are going to say next.

Listen. You'll be one of the three or four business executives out of every hundred who do.

CHAPTER

8

MEETING MANAGEMENT

More meaningful meetings with less meandering

"Giving good meeting" is a WONDERLAND expression. Every executive knows there are good meetings and bad ones, as well as some which are neither good nor bad, just a waste of time.

Meetings exist, according to psychologists, because humans need to be involved in the decision-making process. In a properly conducted meeting, the individual gets this gratification, even if that person expresses no opinion. He or she is part of the process and is able to act in a fashion which controls his or her destiny.

Psychologists also associate the popularity of meetings with the function of group assurance. You are part of the group that is meeting. You are, therefore, an important person. More so than if you were not part of the meeting group. In other words, the meeting bolsters identity, builds ego, and, at the same time, assures an executive of personal worth. Both to him or herself and to the organization.

Meetings can be grand. All too often they are disasters. What makes a good meeting?

Style is one great divider. In order for a manager to be satisfied with the meeting and his or her performance, the style of the meeting must match that of the individual, in a manner that feels emotionally acceptable and assuring. An executive with the CONSERVATORY's careful, sparse use of words might appear cold and distant in a VASTLANDS powwow. The opposite is just as true. A VASTLANDer could look garrulous in a CONSERVATORY boardroom.

Types of businesses also have different styles. A meeting of the creative staff in a New York ad agency is not held along the same lines as a session of a loan committee in a Chicago bank, although both may be talking about the best way to risk millions.

There are definite behaviors for meetings that change with geography and with the nature of the business being discussed.

In all areas but INDUSTRIA, managers and executives feel they attend too many meetings. And that meetings last too long.

General comments on regional meeting practices follow.

CONSERVATORY:

In the land of propriety, Robert's Rules of Order are well understood. As might be expected, meetings here are short, contain no deliberate nonsense, and usually result in decision making. Even if it's only to do further research and reconvene.

Business people here do not complain of meeting length. Then again, complaints from the CONSERVATORY business community to outsiders about anything are rare. To each other, they might display different feelings. But the brevity of most CONSERVATORY conclaves probably alleviates the sense one is spending one's whole career in one meeting or another.

COMMERCIAL CORRIDOR:

Here, life is meeting. Everyone meets, all the time. Long hours spent in meetings, consisting of three or more executives, produces both meeting phobia (meet-phob) and sharp honing of advanced meeting skills (meet-skills). When CORRIDOR executives meet in other regions, their meet-skills, stropped by experience, are devastating. If you don't guard closely against these skills, the CORRIDOR executive will take over your meeting and use it for his/her own purpose.

Meetings here are enthusiastic and aggressive. If there are plum assignments to be taken as next steps, competition runs high. If there exists an opportunity to show superior knowledge of the company, several make the try.

CORRIDOR meetings are seldom relaxed. There is tension, trial, and tribulation. At the end of each session, there is informal scoring to determine who did best, second best, and so on. If you come from outside the CORRIDOR and attend a meeting, be prepared. Both in information on the subject and to stay out of the many lines of fire. You can be shot down in cold blood if you get in the way.

If you come from the CORRIDOR and attend a meeting in another area, lighten up. It's still serious, but there is no need for a kill-or-be-killed attitude.

One fault appears in the CORRIDOR's meeting patterns. Since meetings are a natural way of life, many of the conclaves are really not necessary. They are held to allow a contest of meet-skills, winner take all, which in turn generates meet-phob.

SOUTHLANDS:

A favorite Southern homily holds that while the Yankee generals were meeting and meeting, Lee, Jackson, Beauregard, and old Jubal Early were in the field fighting. If that comes across as a general condemnation of meetings, it is supposed to. Not that Southerners do not enjoy meetings. Next to their counterparts in WONDERLAND, they take meetings with more enjoyment than any other region in the country. It's just that they feel meetings are no substitute for action and generally waste time.

Not that they are against time wasting, either. SOUTH-LANDers simply object to the pretext of meeting to accomplish something when, in reality, everyone is there to pass time.

They're not against pretext, either. It's pretext among friends that is bothersome. Or pretext without purpose. With strangers or for a reason, pretext is well respected.

The above convoluted line of reason/logic is intended to serve as a demonstration of the kind of give-and-take present in a SOUTHLANDS meeting. And to get across the idea executives involved in such meetings enjoy themselves.

SOUTHLANDS meetings are the most relaxed in the nation. In this accomplishment, they outdo even NATURE-LAND. The trouble is, the meetings are so relaxed, often little is achieved.

Meetings in this zone are infrequent. SOUTHLANDers compensate by meeting long. Conferences are seldom called to gain consensus on a matter or direction, but, rather, for a round-table report on the individual actions of those present that touch on the problem under discussion.

SOUTHLANDS meetings have an unofficial but de rigueur format consisting of pre-business discussion amenities lengthy enough to take up three-quarters of the allotted time for the entire conference. This makes meetings fun.

When talk finally turns to business, individuals report on actions they have taken on their own volition, actions they are about to take, or actions they would like to take but, before doing so, require personnel assistance, materials, money, or other aid.

There is little discussion because talking of the actions of another, in a group, could lead to an exchange of insults. If anyone has a question, or (God forbid) a criticism, it is expressed privately to the party involved.

Even Atlanta succumbs to the SOUTHLANDS meeting tradition, despite concerted efforts by outsiders to bring COMMERCIAL CORRIDOR competition into this arena. Submission is probably because Atlanta is the political capital of Georgia, and the southern attitude toward meetings is nowhere better seen than in state capitals.

Outside SOUTHLANDS's urban metropolitan areas, meetings are rare. The boss instructs and all others toil. It doesn't take any meeting to understand that.

INDUSTRIA:

INDUSTRIA is the home of the productive meeting.

That's a definitive statement. Its proof lies in the regional faith which holds that meetings are a means of accomplishing all. In INDUSTRIA, all actions, from new product analysis to corporate organization, are controlled by meetings. What else would you expect when an aggregation of orderly, engineering- or science-trained minds are loosed on a project?

Orderly minds in orderly conduct of business reach orderly conclusions. Precise assignments are made, exact times for reconvening delineated, and the endless process of meeting their way to success is given one more attainable goal.

Most of those who have absorbed engineering or scientific training are accustomed to conforming. Meetings held by and for those who are driven to conform, will be productive meetings. No giant steps will be taken. Progress will be slow. But it is progress and it will be relentless. It's interesting to note that those with technical training who do not conform often make the big breakthroughs, in business as well as in their fields of expertise. This has nothing to do with the subject of meetings in INDUSTRIA, but is an interesting observation nonetheless.

Meetings, in the vernacular of the computer user, drive INDUSTRIA. There are neither too many, nor too few. Either extreme is impossible, as there are as many meetings as needed. No meeting is too short or too long; it lasts for sufficient duration to accomplish that which needed accomplishment.

Meetings drive INDUSTRIA. INDUSTRIA exists to be driven. In an orderly, efficient manner, of course.

Watch yourself if you are from out of the zone and attend a meeting here. Managers are extremely literal. Their idea of pre-business amenities begins and ends with roll call. If you speak concisely when spoken to, do not engage in banter, and, above all, take careful notes, you'll be all right. Slip and you'll instantly be recognized as an outlander.

INDUSTRIAlites who need to attend a meeting in another region must be prepared and show no surprise. Others often tell jokes in meetings and no one jots down the proceedings as if taking notes in class. Do as they do. You know you're smarter than most of them, anyway.

HEARTLAND AMERICA:

What meetings? Bankers have meetings. Insurance people have meetings. Tech folks who sell equipment and fertilizer and other agro-chemicals have meetings. Everyone else in business gets together and "jawbones" about problems.

Meetings are not a productive practice for gregarious folk with a streak of stubborn independence. Even among HEARTLAND businesses which must hold them, meetings have little favor. These are infrequent and short. HEARTLAND executives still complain about the overabundance of, and time consumed in, meetings.

If you come from outside to a meeting here, get your visiting done prior to entering the conference room. ("Howdy in the hallways" is the phrase.) When you sit, be ready for action. If you feel obliged to speak, be direct. Say what you mean to say without small talk. Those present will do the same and hope you appreciate it as much as they do. Their attitude is: "Let's get this over with. I've got work to do."

That one line sums meetings in HEARTLAND. Meetings get in the way of work. They are not onerous in themselves but are an obstacle to be overcome.

VASTLANDS:

The VASTLANDS was home to some of the earliest conventions held in America and some of the wildest conventions ever convened. Since a convention is usually nothing but a group of meetings wrapped around a central theme, this area was long ago a national leader in business meetings.

Of course, none of the fur trappers who came to the rendezvous on the Green River considered himself a businessman or an attendee at a conference. All came to sell their pelts, buy necessities, bet, talk, and get drunk. In other words, to have a good time. It was a chore for these men to make their way through hostile country and Indians to arrive at a site selected a year earlier. To be there on a certain day took true grit. As did living and trapping in snowbound mountains through long cold winters and muddy springs.

Old traditions die hard. Mountain man spirit still lingers in the VASTLANDS and is seen in meeting styles.

Meetings and meals are mixed in other areas. Breakfast is a common time for sales get-togethers across the nation. Luncheon is usually for clients or elite management conferences. Supper or dinner, both regional terms for the final formal meal of the day, is normally reserved for clients or serves as an opportunity for a chief executive from out of town to rally local management, press the flesh, and add a bit of sociability to an otherwise all business visit. (The word "dinner" in parts of the SOUTHLANDS and HEARTLAND means noon meal, not the evening repast. More than one executive has been surprised when asked to "Come to dinner" and a time was provided.)

In the VASTLANDS, meetings and meals go together so often they are almost synonymous. Partly, the practice is caused by the long distance attendees must drive in order to meet. Holding a confab (a common word here) in conjunction with lunch or the evening meal makes sense. Breakfast is also an important conference time, especially since this is an early-to-rise area of the nation. Driving an hour to a seven o'clock breakfast is common.

Another popular conference here is a combination evening meal and meeting with a breakfast meeting the following morning. After the evening session, there is ample time for a few drinks and open discussion of business in a less formal atmosphere. People in the VASTLANDS like less formal atmospheres in business conversations. They become more relaxed and direct in their comments.

VASTLANDS meeting style is casual and flexible. No one seems to mind if participants are called away for phone conversations or paper signing. The flow is broken often by stopping to explain to an absentee who reenters what transpired while he/she was out of the room.

There is an underlying forcefulness, a pressure to get things done. It's seldom expressed through impatience with another attendee, and usually is shown by an individual's taking a hard stand on some matter.

NATURELAND:

Meetings in NATURELAND are normally relaxed and low key. Opening amenities are not unusually long and fall into joke telling.

If there is a point of contention to be discussed, or some problem with one person who will be in the meeting, the wise conference planner usually tries to settle matters in private.

Advance detail work is as common to this area as it is unknown in the COMMERCIAL CORRIDOR, where conflict produced through confrontation allows certain individuals to demonstrate their meet-skill prowess. Advance conferencing is also not well known in INDUSTRIA, where managers would never think to prevent a single issue from dominating the time of an expensive group of executives. In INDUSTRIA, if conflict arises or there is a problem with one individual, the matters are addressed directly, as everyone expects and agrees they should be.

San Francisco meetings, while shorter than those in the COMMERCIAL CORRIDOR, resemble them in style. This must be due to the urban influence and close connections to New York on the part of many companies with offices or affiliates in both cities.

If you attend a NATURELAND meeting, play it straight. You'll hear some rather loquacious speeches, but they'll be balanced by enough shorter ones to make it tolerable. If you feel the need to talk, stay brief. That's not bad advice for a visitor visiting anywhere, but it's especially sage in this zone.

Remember, too, that one type of business, say a bank, and one function of that business, a loan committee for instance, while reflecting meeting habits and attitudes of top executives, will conduct much the same business in any location, coast to coast. The type of loans being evaluated may change, from manufacturing to farmland to refining to oil exploration to timber to real estate, but the evaluation process is much the same. It is not the business conducted. It is the style in which the conducting is done. It's style we are considering here, not content. If you are experienced in a specific business and practice it in one area, your expertise will not be lessened in another, as the principles remain valid.

WONDERLAND:

Where else would Alice go to have such a good time? Where else would she recognize the meeting style as something she

had seen before? The "Caucus Race," a Lewis Carroll creation in which participants chased each other in a circle while
chanting, was endless. Meetings in WONDERLAND are also
thought to be endless. But they have a charm of their own.

WONDERLAND Meeting Mandate Number One: Anything goes.

Each person in attendance is under a compelling obliga-
tion to direct the meeting in such a fashion as to attain from
those present precisely what he or she desires. Extra points
are awarded if you can get what you want and at the same
time keep someone else from getting what he/she wants. If
you can keep yet another from getting part of his/her goal,
half the number of extra points are yours. Give a meeting
where anyone in attendance gets what he/she wants, and that
person will say, "You give good meeting." As an accolade,
it's a bit of a black mark. It indicates to others that to meet
with you is not a fate worse than death. Your best has been
bested.

This leads to Mandate Two: No matter what happens in
a meeting, no matter if you win or lose, you must make
everyone believe the end result is precisely the outcome for
which you were striving. It may take considerable manipu-
lation of facts, as well as consummate acting ability, but is
worth the effort. Once you are able to carry off the decep-
tion, it will appear you never lose. More, you gain the reputation of having a devious mind. A highly praised asset in
WONDERLAND.

MEXICA:

MEXICA meetings are not so complex as in other areas. Recall that this is the land machismo built and you'll have the
precise behavior for successful meeting attendance. Part of
the macho code is seemingly not to care about the acts of
others. So no matter what happens, do not appear concerned. You may, if you wish, look reasonably interested in
the proceedings. However, this guise takes some practice,

so those from out of the zone should attempt it only if they are meeting experts on their home turf.

Power meetings, in which individuals, by showing their meet-skills, dominate the proceedings and look good to their superiors, are rare. Such an action cannot occur when superiors are judging each other's reactions from behind identical shields of indifference.

WASHINGTON, D.C.:

The less said about meetings in Washington, the better. Let's leave it at that.

MIAMI:

With demeanors more disinterested than those seen in MEXICA, the only way a Miami conference can get cooler would be to hold it in a refrigerator.

Do not attend a meeting of Cuban businessmen (even though all may speak excellent English) without an interpreter. You'll lose out on a lot of fascinating byplay. A fiscal allocation to buy a gross of pencils brings on as much histrionics, pro and con, as the decision to finance a new office building. It's not the importance of the matter. It's the feelings of the executives arguing the matter that count.

An overview of all regions reveals an interesting similarity among meeting mavens. Even though this book deals with differences in behavior across the U.S., these similarities are worthy of inclusion.

Those with incisive meet-skills seem to be classifiable into three groups. There are Note Takers, Summer-Uppers, and Next-Steppers.

Note Takers do precisely what the name implies. They take copious notes on proceedings. Some write everything that transpires. Others focus on points of agreement. Savvy

Note Takers record each participant's principal position and watch closely for digressions. They know where everyone stands at the end of the session. This allows siding with either the winning opinions or, in a contest between managers, the best side for advancement. By reference to their notes later, they can see the development of an idea, acceptance of a previously rejected option, or the creation of a new possibility as it forms. Notes help them excel in future meetings with those same upper management executives present.

Summer-Uppers attempt to shine by appearing to slice through endless rhetoric and stating positions of others. Not their own, but positions for each person in the room. (Whether they have one or not.) The Summer-Upper never personally assumes a position, and while delineating others' positions takes great care not to identify with any stance. Often, the position he/she ascribes so grandly to you or your side in the argument is not your position at all. But once verbalized, it becomes your position, and if you have any smarts, you'd best drop your previous view and begin defending the one now ascribed to you, or you will look pretty foolish. An expert riposte to the Summer-Upper is two-fold:

A. As you defend your newly assigned views, gently come back into line with your original views. That's hard, but it might be easier than the next response.

B. Force the Summer-Upper to take a stand. There is nothing so frightening to the Summer-Upper as being forced to take a position.

If you can achieve this once in ten times, your meet-skills need no further honing. With three in ten, you are a meeting menace, and no one, from the chairperson of your company down, should ever meet with you or without you, depending upon circumstances.

Summer-Uppers are a phenomenon east of the Mississippi River, but can occur coast to coast. They are more indigenous to large cities than smaller communities.

The Next-Stepper uses a ploy based on the idea that it's not dangerous to take charge after decisions have been made. This individual lies in wait, saying little, until all have gained concurrence. Then, with the speed of light, the Next-Stepper begins delineating work needed to be done to implement decisions and assigning, by indirect request, work to be completed prior to the next conference.

No successful Next-Stepper is lazy. When work assignments are made, he or she clearly demonstrates an eagerness to tackle a tough task, albeit a task for which the Next-Stepper is personally well suited. Or one which has, unbeknownst to others attending the meeting, already been done. Rivals of Next-Steppers who do not stay alert discover themselves in a situation where they either agree to the most onerous projects or appear to be uncooperative and discordant.

The Next-Stepper gambit can usually be recognized by the following pattern:

Next-Stepper: "Let's see. Well, several items need to be handled. I'll take care of rewriting the Wobjensky report. Sara, will you have all the figures on the trade-in scheme?"

Sara: "Well, I . . ."

N-S: "Great. Knew we could count on you. Pete . . ."

Watch for the sequence. It goes: Say there is work to be done, take on a large task, then assign others rapidly. Shocking how often such a simple trick works. Especially with those in the VASTLANDS and NATURELAND, where managers are more relaxed and feel that if someone wants to take charge, that person must have a reason.

A polished Next-Stepper can appear, without having made a single contribution to a meeting, to have chaired the whole discussion. A truly skilled N-S can also leave the feeling that without his/her input, the meeting would have been a shambles of indecision.

In summation, while there are well-documented points of similarity in meeters and meeting styles across the nation, regional variances exist and play an important role in the decision-making process. Knowing how the game is played in different areas can enhance your success.

CHAPTER

9

CLOTHING CONCEPTS

Dressing for success
has regionalities

"Clothes do not the man make" is a Victorian English senti-
ment that applies to those of the feminine gender as well. It
can be taken to mean a slattern, dressed as a lady, is still a
slattern. Or a gentleman, dressed as a poverty-stricken der-
elict, will still be a gentleman. That it was necessary to present the observation at all shows humans have judged peers
by their clothing and appearance for a long time.

In today's business world, clothes may not make the man
or woman, but they exert tremendous influence on career
success. A number of tomes written on the importance of
dress in business, especially those produced in recent years,
give clear instructions on correct styles and fashions as if there
is a single U.S. standard.

Well, there is, more or less, a single, nationally agreed
upon manager-executive uniform. For the male, it consists
of a dark suit and black over-the-calf socks worn with black
shoes, preferably with laces in an oxford style. A white shirt
is de rigueur (although there is some argument as to whether
or not white should be worn before 6:00 P.M., so blue is
acceptable). The tie is selected either to blend in (darker

tones) or stand out (red, yellows, and brighter colors). Use of patterned fabrics for suits, aside from pinstripes, should not be encouraged. Male accessories must be sparse and preferably have some relationship to business. A gold pen, for instance, never worn in a pocket where it will show, and a gold wristwatch, worn on the left hand, are ideal. Wedding rings are permissible. Other rings are not.

Businesswomen may accessorize and bejewel, but never bedazzle. One group holds that since females are feminine, they should appear feminine. A second view maintains a unisex stance and encourages, as far as physical differences allow, identical appearances in both men and women.

The popular dark suit, consisting of jacket and skirt with a white or pastel blouse and integral tie at the neck (which may be fixed in a bow), is frequently seen. The outfit is completed by medium-heeled shoes, natural shade hose, and limited, simple jewelry. (Businesswomen who dress in this direction have returned to the old "point" system as taught in Charm School during the 1950s. Each eye-catching accessory or gem is awarded one point. A bright scarf at the neck, for example, is one point, as is a large diamond ring or gold wristwatch. Three "points" is maximum when wearing the unisex solution to business dress. Two points is a better score for daily office wear.)

Simple, tailored dresses, more feminine suits, or a skirt/blouse from the unisex suit, without jacket, are only three of many other possibilities. Women have much wider range in dressing their bodies in executive-acceptable clothing than do men. Even with that range, a national standard does exist, although there are notable variances.

Alongside the national norm are several purely regional styles that are quite acceptable in the areas where they have developed. One would not be out of place, going from sea to shining sea, in the Dark Suit Standard. One would appear oddly dressed in any of the various regional uniforms outside home territory.

Regional clothing styles have their place and express definite aspects of a business person's personality. In analyzing distinct regional variations in dress, it quickly becomes clear that not every region has a difference in business dress generally accepted as an alternative throughout the business community, and that several regions have more than one. The simplest way to examine these phenomena is on the basis of clothing style.

Every part of the United States, Europe, most of the Orient, and Soviet Union, too, judging from the popularity of American-made jeans, went through a "western" (meaning Nashville country and western music and dancing) dress craze. Movies hyped it, TV stereotyped it, restaurants themed on it, and blue jean manufacturers, accustomed to selling thousands of pairs of rugged pants to students and hardworking men, suddenly faced a demand from both sexes that soared into the millions.

At first, base price items were acceptable. Then, as clever product makers realized the intensity of this boom and began to manufacture especially for new buyers, the ante was raised. Striving to find a marketable difference that would allow a sensible person, especially females, to pay five times the normal price for a pair of tight fitting denim trousers became standard. The fit trick was rapidly followed by prestige labeling and, finally, by obvious external markings on the pants to show they cost more than the competition.

As an aside, please try to imagine the surprise of the rather staid manufacturers as they found their durable work pants in demand. All they could do was hang on and hope the bubble didn't burst as profits soared. Mills had to reset to produce more of the coarse blue fabric, and cutters added extra shifts.

The only similar situation in modern business during the last three decades was the overnight, shocking increase in sales of roll-your-own cigarette papers that began in the 1960s. Business increased and new brands appeared in what had been a failing, stagnant product category. The last big boom in cigarette papers had come with the 1930s Depression, when "tailormade" cigarettes were too expensive for average working stiffs, so they had to roll their own. Top executives in the cigarette paper companies must have suffered sleepless nights wondering whether or not to sell their stocks and bonds, since sales of their product were so clearly linked to periods of financial disaster. Minds probably rested easier when it was learned it was only dope smoking that caused the increases.

Blue jeans are not the western wear considered correct for business, except in isolated communities in MEXICA, NATURELAND, the VASTLANDS, and HEARTLAND. Even in these retreats, which accept the attire, no one actually believes it is correct. Some do it out of necessity; others from cussedness. (Clerical types, male and female, do wear them to the office in all zones. Managers and executives should not.) During the early boom, WONDERLAND management wore jeans in the office, but this practice rapidly declined.

There are, however, two types of western clothing styles that are emotionally acceptable and correct throughout these areas. The first consists of trousers and jacket cut from a heavy khaki material. Pants are jeanlike, with straight or tapering legs and front but no side pockets. Jackets are similar to nylon shells, and many zip as opposed to button. These items are worn with a tailored shirt, usually white, with pearl-buttoned snap pockets. A wide tooled-leather belt with a large buckle, and square-toe cowboy boots complete the look. (Originally, these boots had sharp toes and high heels so the rider's foot would easily engage a stirrup, yet not so easily slip through, a condition that all too often resulted in the rider being dragged by a heel behind the horse.) This outfit is favored by farmers, ranchers, oil executives, and other outdoor businessmen. A past president of the United States wore it frequently.

·

The female counterpart is identical, except for the option of a skirt. More women today are simply altering the cut of pants to better suit their shapes and have forsworn the skirt. This costume is considered to be in good taste at all daytime and many evening functions, from board meetings to dinner at a pricey restaurant.

The outfit, for both men and women, is usually topped with a western style hat. In hot weather, jackets may be discarded, exposing shirt sleeves. Men usually show a bulge on their hip, where they pocket their wallets.

The second western style is seen more in the larger cities of MEXICA, the VASTLANDS, and HEARTLAND. This is a suit, again with skirt or trouser option for females, cut along lines referred to euphemistically as "western." Shoulders are broad, the jacket body hangs straight, there are patch side pockets, and overall, a special embroidery piping or trim makes curls and loops for decoration. Hat, belt, buckle, and boots complement the look. Tight, tapered trousers with pockets as seen in jeans complete the outfit. Neckwear can be an open shirt, with perhaps a scarf for a touch of formality; or a silver-tipped neck rope clamped under the chin by a turquoise and silver slide. This dress, observed frequently in major cities of the areas mentioned, is considered proper. Some outlanders view it as eccentric, but those who wear it see no reason to subscribe to a national "norm" and have been raised in places where this style is recognized as correct.

Transplant one of these businessmen or women from a mid-size town to the wilds of New York City, and he/she will often take offense at the commotion made over his/her clothes. After all, a New Yorker's dress isn't strange to them.

An interesting effect, stemming partially from the western influence, is the decreasing number of men in all areas who wear cuffs in their trousers. No western outfits ever have cuffs, unless it's the turn-up caused by purchasing a pair of jeans in too long a leg length. When the no-cuff style was introduced from Europe to men's sports clothes, it seemed almost effeminate. Now, it's the norm. The next time you board an aircraft and are seated, watching fellow passengers file past, focus on trouser bottoms. Check how widespread the no-cuff style is today.

Earlier mention of the no-coat, shirt-only, warm-weather option brings up two additional styles based on the absence of a coat. Both of these are quite correct in their home areas, and both have spread somewhat in the U.S. during the last few years.

In the WONDERLAND belt, and extending as far as Las Vegas, daytime style, also seen at night with the addition of a lightweight, white jacket, is a fine-fabric, open-neck shirt with one or more gold chains as neckwear. Light color, light-weight trousers complete the ensemble. No one can see a belt, as the shirt is worn outside the trousers. If it is tucked in, slacks are preferably those which require no belt and have no belt loops. Sleeves on shirts may be rolled or neatly buttoned at the cuff. The weight of gold at the throat should not be sufficient to cause difficulty with movement or force the head to bow under the load.

Variations on this theme include loud-patterned "aloha" shirts in vibrant colors. This Hawaiian addition has proven itself and is finding growing acceptance. Outside the executive suite.

It is not unusual to attend a meeting in WONDERLAND and discover dress ranging from American Normal to WON-DERLAND Relaxed (shirt look above) and every nuance in between. Many professionals have adopted this shirt style while many of those, not professional but who wish to appear so, have gone the suit and tie route. The theory, apparently, is: Dress as you wish to be perceived. In WONDERLAND, others will play along. They don't want you bursting their bubble either.

The other coatless style is akin to the Hawaiian aloha shirt as the antecedent of the multihued beauty evolved from the "wedding" shirt seen in the Philippines. Similar in cut, but of a solid color using tucks and buttons for decoration, the Spanish-influenced, Philippine garment is predecessor, or possibly successor, of the "guayabera" tradition.

Guayabera is the most common name for the long- and short-sleeved shirt sported by Latin businessmen in tropical countries. A traditional guayabera has four pockets and rows of pleats down both sides of the chest. Extra buttons are sewn at junctions of some seams to give a decorative effect. Normally white, these graceful shirts, which are worn loose, not tucked into trousers, now come in a multitude of colors. No tie is needed, and in fact the collar is not tailored to accept one. White is still the choice for a more formal office, and the long-sleeved model is preferred for evening use.

The guayabera is cool to wear, looks neat, and is fully accepted for all types of business meetings. Coupled with a dark pair of slacks, dark socks, and black shoes, the outfit is the equivalent of the American Standard Business Suit.

Guayaberas long ago captured Miami by storm. Anglos and Latins alike wear them. Penetration into MEXICA began earlier, but took several generations longer. Now, though, the sight of this shirt is common, especially in San Antonio, El Paso, and points west. They are also starting to appear in certain parts of New York City, although the climate there, for many months, is far too cold for this style to be comfortable.

The guayabera has not yet attained the level of acceptability throughout the business community in MEXICA as has been gained by the western suit. In all likelihood, it will, especially if a new energy shortage forces the cost of air conditioning upwards.

Another form of garb, similar to the Standard American Suit, is found predominately in the SOUTHLANDS. In place of heavier fabrics of the North, seersucker and thin wale corduroy are cut into lightweight outfits along traditional lines. Colors run toward blue and ecru.

This kind of summerwear has made inroads elsewhere, notably in San Francisco, where "traditional" tailoring is popular. They are also seen in the COMMERCIAL CORRIDOR, Boston, and a small portion of the CONSERVATORY. Latest improvements in synthetic-natural fiber blends, grouped together as "wash and wear," have made these lightweights increasingly more wrinkle resistant. They provide a fresh, crisp appearance and, if not comfortable on the hottest days, at least are superior to wool in those conditions. (Interestingly enough, visitors moving north from the SOUTHLANDS and MEXICA often complain of low temperatures inside buildings. It can get cold wearing a cotton jacket in an office where the comfort zone is set for executives dressed in heavier fabrics.)

One final style, found mostly in the VASTLANDS but also pronounced in NATURELAND, has no counterpart in the balance of the U.S. Many business people, both males and females, have begun dressing in a fashion that, for want of a better name, can be termed "Outdoor-Rugged." Professionals, too, have joined this trend. In fact, physicians and attorneys probably started it.

Outdoor-Rugged is a combination of well-worn (read: almost worn out), expensive, brand-name, rough-country clothes, some form of lace-up boots, and for men, a certain hirsuteness caused by going too long between haircuts and shaving every third day. Women in the same look have their hair casually but perfectly done. They do not look as if they've gone too long between shaves.

Accessories include a gold waterproof wristwatch, a Jappanese wrist chronometer, or a new, but old-fashioned pocket watch. The left breast pocket of the shirt (men only) contains at least two, but preferably three, pens. Either the most expensive gold brands or the cheapest plastic throwaways.

Clothes are layered on the body. Above a pair of Filson "iron pants" goes a lightweight cotton work shirt, usually blue, a knitted sweater, and an armless goose-down vest. That may sound a bit much for the summer, but seldom in the affairs of man or woman has chic fashion been dictated by seasonal climatic vagaries. Style, yes; fashion, no.

Wearers of such garb place great effort into the selection of proper boots. New lightweight high-top climbers made by various running shoe manufacturers are popular, as is the standard logging boot minus spikes imbedded in the soles like golf shoes. (In logging country, those spikes, called calks, pronounced "corks," are standard footwear. Loggers are careful, needless to say, how they step indoors.)

Shirts of plain cotton should never, never sport epaulets and must always have flaps which snap or button in place over each pocket.

There is an interesting power statement in the "rugged" look. Worn to a board meeting, it implies the wearer is sufficiently self-assured to dress comfortably. This shows, in effect, what a natural chap he really is and, at the same time, demonstrates improved status from that quantum time when he had to appear in Standard American Business Garb. Since this attitude is in keeping with the mores of both the VAST-LANDS and NATURELAND, the dress style, while not pleasing to older executives, is acceptable.

Note that, as unfair as it might be, only male executives wear this garb to business functions. Females below the managerial level often arrive in the office dressed in some variation of the "rugged" outfit. It is not unusual in the COMMERCIAL CORRIDOR or INDUSTRIA, either. Cold climates and exposure to elements while traveling to and from the work place make this a practical outfit. It was, after all, developed by those who work out-of-doors every day in the year. Secretaries may look this way. Clerks may look this way. Upwardly directed females may not. Especially in VAST- and NATURELANDs.

It is a fascinating observation, as well as being true, that across our nation, the more informally male executives dress, the more formally female executives are required to dress.

In the CONSERVATORY, everyone is formal. In manner and clothing. In the COMMERCIAL CORRIDOR, male executives are formal. Less so than in the CONSERVATORY, but more so than in INDUSTRIA. Female executives are expected to be reasonably formal in dress as well. A certain degree of casualness is more than acceptable.

In INDUSTRIA, males are less formal, and females more so than in the CORRIDOR. Most of the casualness is gone, and there is a trend toward uniform styles.

In HEARTLAND, men are less formal; women more. In the SOUTHLANDS, the same is true, with the women being a degree more formal than in HEARTLAND or INDUSTRIA.

In NATURELAND and the VASTLANDS, male executives are quite informal, but no female executive would ever wear slacks or jeans to the office. In fact, tailored suits are preferred to dresses and, in an effort to image for success, the female is forced into at least the same degree of formality as seen in the SOUTHLANDS, and more than is usual for the CORRIDOR.

Please note the above applies only to women attaining management levels. And, naturally, those who aspire to do so.

Other regional differences in clothing styles center on suit cut, personal jewelry, ties, belts, shoes, and suspenders. A quick overview will provide a clear picture of dressing for business in America.

One would not believe the cut of suits could vary as much as it does in the U.S. After all, a limited number of manufacturers make ninety percent of all men's suits sold nationwide. The same brands are found in every major city and the same size structure is applied in every line. A top name suit in size 40-Long will be the same from Maine to California. Right? To a point only.

Suits are an unusual retail item in that they come incomplete and it is up to the selling clothier to finish them. Jackets are altered, trouser waist and crotch are resewn, and legs are adjusted for correct length. The outcome is a semi-custom product produced after the sale of the original stock suit.

Leaving out individual lapses of good taste, personal feeling about loud or muted colors, and a visual good sense not to mix stripes with stripes or commit other grotesqueries, here, in a quick scan, are readily visible regional differences in style.

CONSERVATORY:

Suits are cut a little fuller, more in the "sack" shape. Shoulders receive little or no padding. Ties are knotted so the length assures the tip extends below the belt. Jewelry is held to a minimum. Suspenders are not a fad. Three buttons on the coat, please. No sport coats in business. Lace shoes, although tassel loafers are permissible.

COMMERCIAL CORRIDOR:

European influence produces a fitted look, even in sack styles. Tie tips below belts. Jewelry is acceptable, but not in excess. Suspenders wax and wane, but are viewed as an accessory rather than a necessity. Two buttons on jackets unless the wearer is a traditionalist. Sport coats are occasionally permitted. Slip-on shoes, in the moccasin style, are normal.

SOUTHLANDS:

Suits are loosely cut. Trousers break over shoe tops. Ties are wider and end above the belt. Belts are wider, too. Jewelry is favored, and class rings are common. Suspenders, often with a belt, too, for the older set. Sport coat and slacks okay. Shoes are optional. In style, that is. (Bare feet, while "in" in some places in the SOUTHLANDS, are "out" in the executive suite.)

INDUSTRIA:

Trousers are straight-legged and have a pronounced break. Suits are neither fitted nor loose. They are the economy-model in between. Ties end at the belt line. Belts are wider than in the CORRIDOR. Class rings abound. Pens and pencils jut from coat and shirt pockets. Sport coats and slacks are often worn in place of a suit. What suspenders? No set shoe style.

HEARTLAND:

Bagginess is the word, and poor fit, with stuffed shoulders and full seats the norm. Executive Chicago has the style of the CORRIDOR; the rest of HEARTLAND looks rural. Ties end a button above the belt and are often clamped to the shirt front with an ornate clip. Trousers break deeply. Suspenders are often seen, but not for style. The wider belt of heavy leather with a larger buckle is most common. Jewelry, aside from a wedding ring and gold watch, and possibly a class ring, is not seemly. Since, after all, a coat and tie is a coat and tie, sport jackets are often worn as suits would be in the CORRIDOR. Heavy shoes are common, as are boots.

VASTLANDS:

Suits here are a cross between HEARTLAND and CORRIDOR. A little better fitted, but not as well done as in the CORRIDOR. Break in trousers a must; tie ends above a belt that is ornate and made to be noticed. Class rings are standard. Other jewelry, except for silver Indian crafts, is not common. Suspenders are a curiosity. Boots are usual footwear.

NATURELAND:

Suits are conservative. Even the most expensive have been altered to look like mid-price-range specials. Trousers are a bit baggy with a small break; belts follow the VASTLANDS pattern, but are not quite so noticeable; and jewelry, aside from wedding ring, watch, and class ring, is verboten. Ties end at the beltline. Boots are seen, but shoes are more common.

WONDERLAND:

Who knows? Every style and alteration known to man, from Deep South Sunday Meeting Stump Orator through Acrimonious, Parsimonious CONSERVATORY Banker. And back again. Jewelry? None, to everything you own or can borrow, lease, or rent. Plus sunglasses.

MEXICA:

The basic American HEARTLAND suit altered to be tighter in every place a tuck can be taken, and/or the latest Continental, nip-waisted, shorter-sleeved, tight-trouser ensembles. Wide belts with noticeable buckles. Ties end at belt top. A heavy, gold Rolex wristwatch is the norm. Class and wedding rings encouraged. Other limited jewelry permissible. Boots are typical. If not, slip-on loafers.

Mentioned earlier is the new American trend to cuffless trousers. The shift from cuffed to cuffless is in full stride, but cuffs still have favor among upper echelon executives unless they have adopted tighter Continental styles.

Throughout the nation, businessmen in rural areas tend to wear pointed-toe cowboy boots with their business suits. Their ties stop higher above belt lines than those of their city cousins, and jewelry, aside from a watch and class ring, is less favored. Synthetic fabrics that look synthetic are more common among this group.

It is possible, with only a little study, to classify businessmen and, to a lesser degree, women, into strata. Those in top management positions show reasonable regional variation in dress. It is present, but softened. Those in mid-to-upper management ranges show considerably more variance, and those in lower managerial plateaus demonstrate remarkable regional differences. Part of the wide range is due to money, still more to opportunity for cross contact.

Using the preceding pages, observe business travelers. You will be surprised at dress variations. Take a guess at each person's place of origin, then ask. You'll be astounded how often you are correct.

Regional influences that cause variations in clothes also apply to the wearing of those clothes, as well. There are definite body mannerisms among the population of an area that influence how a coat and trousers, or a jacket and skirt, or a dress, fit the human frame. Since these are indigenous to and endemic in a given population, at least part of this influence must trickle into executive offices. This effect is reflected in an old saying:

"You may take the boy out of the country, but you can't take the country out of the boy."

The same truth holds for adults of both sexes. And urbanites, as well.

CHAPTER

10

A POTPOURRI OF DEFINABLE DIFFERENCES

Of matters sensual, alcoholic, and clubby

We've exposed some differences in executive behavior by covering the U.S. on an area basis while considering regional variations in a variety of subjects.

There are several more topics which, while reflecting strong regional bias, are much like one MEXICA executive's description of rivers. The rivers are, he said, "a mile wide and a foot deep, with water too thick to drink but too thin to plow." In other words, these topics are too large to simply ignore, yet too small or insufficiently widespread to merit individual chapters.

Nonetheless, these deserve at least passing attention. As opposed to a region-by-region presentation, subjects will be named and, in a short discussion, the regions that have variance from the whole, enumerated.

TALKING SEX:

One of the banes of female executives is the traditional business pastime of talking sex. In the days before women assumed a role in the executive work force, an all male staff enjoyed daily discourse on a number of subjects. Two, sports and sex, were popular and considered a male prerogative.

Sports talk threw off many expressions that in some parts of the U.S. became descriptions of business activities. One company "blitzed" another. It might be deemed better to "walk" a competitor, rather than take a chance he might "knock one in the cheap seats." A vice-president "K.O.'d" his opponent, and had him "on the ropes."

Sports-based jargon, readily understood by most men, was foreign to the female and caused concern. Enough so that to this day, in certain segments of the country, women aspiring to be in, or already in, managerial ranks, take courses on Power Talking, the language of the executive suite.

Sex talk is a vital topic in these instructional programs. Traditionally, sexually oriented jokes and talk of sex are an accepted conversational pastime among male management. This is probably also true of those in business at lesser levels, but in agreement with national studies showing that better educated men have more direct conversations about matters sexual, the practice appears to intensify from middle management upwards. All the way to the top.

As women entered the work force and began assuming management positions, their presence in what had been an all male environment was felt in many ways. Sex talk was one area in which there was immediate conflict. Men shut their mouths, which made for awkward moments. Imagine entering a room for a meeting, and the second you are recognized, the speaker, possibly turning red in the face, abruptly stops. You can feel the anticipation which came, unknown to you, from the proximity of the punchline of the almost-told joke. There is an embarrassed silence for a moment, then someone, out of desperation, addresses you innocuously. Sex talk in the office has clearly undergone some changes.

Upper management and higher levels in the professions are still male dominated. This means (since the process of advancement is, to a large extent, a system of winnowing away those who, for one reason or another, are unsuited for management in a particular firm) there are more males at middle level positions than females. Far more. And since midrange positions are staffed by those in their late twenties to late thirties, a period among humans when sexuality is relatively high and combines well with early adult independence, sex talk is normal.

Females are traditionally excluded from male sex talk, as are males from similar discussions among females. That sentence is not quite correct because sex talk in male groups is not "similar," aside from base subject, to that in female groups. But as the French have been quoted as saying, "Vive la difference!"

What does a lone female assigned to a task team of ten males do when sex talk starts? Or when it's started and she causes conversationalis interruptus? Here is where regional differentiation shows.

In the SOUTHLANDS, she does nothing. She does not join in; she does not acknowledge the subject of conversation which may flow about her. She is a rock. A demure rock, but a rock nonetheless. (Leave out Atlanta. Atlanta follows the next mode.) SOUTHLANDS males are used to talking around their women, so it makes little difference to them. They do watch their words, to abridge any overly salacious or descriptive phrases, and they curtail jokes. At best, they have reached an uneasy truce, based on traditional sex roles.

In the COMMERCIAL CORRIDOR, INDUSTRIA, and VASTLANDS, two female trends appear to have emerged. The first can be summed up by the phrase, "One of the Gang." The girls have abandoned, as much as possible, their learned female responses, and have moved to become one of the group. This has switched the phrase "One of the Boys" to "One of the Gang."

If a guy makes a sexually oriented comment concerning the pleasure he might receive from a certain act, the girl is easily able to relate that to her own sexual satisfaction and agree enthusiastically. Without acquiescence to actual physical contact. If that sounds difficult to carry off, remember: Females have been handling sexual interest of males for a long time now. They possess a body of instinctive, if not hereditary, knowledge.

An example of One of the Gang dialogue goes as follows: "Wow, Joan! You look terrific today. Good enough to eat."

"Sounds terrific, but don't make promises you can't keep."

"I'd keep it if you'd let me."

"I'll keep it if your wife'll let you. Bring me a note."

"I don't need a note. Eatin' ain't cheatin'."

"It is in my book. But thanks for the invitation."

As can be seen, the female has successfully competed in sex banter with a male.

Another, more crude dialogue shows participation in sexually oriented language by the female.

Male: (discussing a report) "What's your reaction?"

Female: "Well, if worse comes to worst, we can always just pay them."

Male: "Fuck that."

Female: "Sounds kind of kinky to me, but I'll watch while you try."

Being One of the Gang deals with the problem on an interesting level. Both examples, by the way, are verbatim, overheard during the normal course of a business day. A third example, also crude and also real, will suffice to show that in this mode it is possible for the female to completely enter into the language as well as the spirit.

Male: (to a female employee) "Lookin' good today, darlin'."

Female: "Don't give me that 'darlin'' crap. I've got a name."

Male: "I like 'em feisty, Barbara."

Female: "Great."

Male: "No kiddin'. I'd like to get in your pants."

Female: "Now what would I do with two assholes?"

The above illustrations show the extent to which becoming One of the Gang has progressed.

The other alternative, quite common in some areas, is the "Freeze." In the hands of the right female, it is a stunning statement of independence.

Male: "Nice blouse, Miss Tilly." (If a woman is known for doing the Freeze, no one will use her first name in the office.)

Female: (after freezing for a second; that is, stopping all movement and staring at the male) "Personal remarks have no place in an office, Mr. James."

The Freeze is now complete, and as soon as mutual embarrassment subsides, the two can return to productive work. A good Freezer can appear to avoid being embarrassed and deliver the line so devastatingly as to render the male speechless for moments.

Neither the Freeze nor One of the Gang will work in the CONSERVATORY. Not because the concepts are ineffective, but because there is no need for them. There is indeed no place for sex in the office. In upper echelons of traditional CONSERVATORY executive hierarchy, innuendo and rumor hold there may be no place for sex at all. There are still small towns where pregnant women only come out of their homes before dawn or in late evening because it's plain to see from looking at them what they've been doing.

Not all CONSERVATORY executive offices are sexless, of course, but even the most liberal are almost Victorian by contrast to parts of America.

HEARTLAND females use the Freeze (albeit in milder form) but not the One of the Gang techniques. Their softening of the Freeze to "Don't be silly, Tom. We've got work to do," is more than ample for this region.

The Gang ploy is too strong to even contemplate using in HEARTLAND. Efforts to implement it might end a lady in jail. Or under mental observation.

WONDERLAND managers have developed a cunning solution. They had to, as there is more between-sexes sex talk in upper level WONDERLAND offices than in most houses of prostitution. And more straight talk on the subject by females, too. Exchange between the sexes is so great the problem has simply ceased to exist for natives. WONDER-LAND ladies no longer feign to recognize there ever was a difficulty, which makes for interesting reactions from outsiders suddenly placed in this environment.

COMMERCIAL CORRIDOR female executives, especially those from New York City, are well able to give a good accounting for themselves in this matter. Since the movement for women in management positions began there, they have had more time than many to overcome the last vestiges of traditional role shyness.

Women of MEXICA recognize the problem in the larger cities. In smaller communities, there is no problem. It is against the macho code for males to behave in such a fashion before ladies. Sex talk is performed out of female earshot. And that's that.

Well, not quite. A multifaceted conflict is developing in Houston, San Antonio, Phoenix, and Dallas. In these cities, executive sex talk between both sexes is not uncommon in the office. Females control it with judicious use of a modified Freeze and some even resort to the Gang, a defense which is spreading.

Office groups, especially younger mid-management folks, carry this same sex banter into the bars of MEXICA, where they congregate for an after-work aperitif. Their talk is overheard by those who would not, under any circumstances, discuss such matters in mixed company. This gives rise to some interesting conflicts.

The Freeze modification in MEXICA is: "Come on, Bob. We can't be friends if you talk like that." It seems to work well.

Office sex talk is a standard business practice. The influence of females in managerial ranks has dampened the activity, but it is far from abolished. Since trends traditionally travel east from WONDERLAND across the nation, techniques seen there are likely to become standard. This means use of colorful language will increase for a few years until everyone sees both boys and girls doing it, then peak, and fall dramatically. In a decade, even HEARTLANDers are liable to be wondering what the fuss was all about.

BUSINESS AND ALCOHOL:

No one knows precisely where the phrase "three-martini lunch" was coined. Most attribute it to the mighty brain of a Washington, D.C. PR person, who coined it in support of a tax proposal. The three-martini meal existed at one time. And may still, in some places, among some people. For most managers in the decade of the '8os, it's a passé tradition. In fact, the custom has almost ceased to exist.

Total consumption of alcoholic beverages in the U.S. has dropped as well. This is the logical outcome of a pair of trends now more than twenty years old.

The fitness fixation began mildly enough with a tennis boom, meandered into running, and now embraces all manner of high-exertion physical activity. "Flat bellies" became the clarion call of Baby Boomers inexorably becoming thirty, then forty, and facing fifty. A natural outgrowth of muscular conditioning was whole-system tune-ups, with focus on systemic harm from smoking cigarettes and imbibing alcohol.

Preferences in hard liquor began to change. Old stand-bys, which had dominated sales since shortly after the end of prohibition, began to give way to "clear" liquor. In other words, the bourbon and scotch bunch fell to the vodka valiants. The light trend spread from whiskey to wines, leaving reds in progressively more disfavor, then to beer, where a new category was formed, then back to "hard" beverages, where for the second round, many began to abstain or reduce intake. Sparkling waters appeared and proliferated, as soft drink sales made them smile in Atlanta.

In the face of all this, executives in large numbers still drink at noon. The switch from a scotch and soda to a glass of white wine may have been made, but alcohol is still being consumed, albeit in smaller amounts.

Consumption is not equal across the nation. And not equal in terms of age, either. Older executives continue to consume more than younger counterparts. This was true when the older men and women were the younger set, but there is a difference today.

Today's middle manager is an advocate of a health-oriented lifestyle. Flabbies and out-of-winds still exist in good numbers, but the trend is to no smoking, white wine as the strongest alcoholic beverage, and that in moderation, and a low diet. A "low" diet is one low in fats, triglycerides, and cholesterol. Two of those three words weren't even familiar to most physicians twenty years ago.

At lunch with the boss, a glass of wine is the cocktail. At lunch with peers, sparkling water serves the same purpose. At home a glass of white vino is the preferred beverage. Along with an assortment of sugar-free soft drinks, fruit juices, and tea. Coffee is consumed only as espresso, and not all that often.

As these individuals move upward in their careers, they are less likely to tipple as much strong booze as their predecessors. So the example they set for those coming behind will be more abstemious than that set for them. Where this cycle will end, no one knows. Booze will not be abolished, but consumption, among executives of tomorrow, will most assuredly be less than among those in similar positions yesterday.

Reduction of alcoholic intake is seen in the COMMERCIAL CORRIDOR among the same groups. No prohibition exists against a noon shooter or two. It's just an inclination on the part of the younger executives.

A gentlemanly cocktail at noon has long been a practice in the CONSERVATORY. A ladylike cocktail has been added. No change is seen here, except again, the younger group is following the lighter, healthier trend.

INDUSTRIA is the land of hard drinking. Not the exuberant imbibing seen in VASTLANDS, but a more concerted consumption. The national trend toward lightness is here, but it's seen in a shift from bourbon or scotch to vodka and rum, instead of from 80 proof spirits to 14 percent wine. Executives drink at noon, at happy hour after work, in the evening, and on weekends. If the three-martini business lunch lingers, it is here, not in an elegant Manhattan restaurant. And it's liable to be in the form of a six-ounces-in-one-glass noontime special drink, used by restaurants to lure the lunch bunch.

As INDUSTRIA executives imbibe, the SOUTHLANDS go dry. Communities here and in parts of HEARTLAND did not sell alcohol, aside from beer and wine, by the drink, across a bar, until the 1970s. Many still have state-controlled liquor stores and stringent laws concerning public consumption.

In the SOUTHLANDS, there is a religious resistance to alcohol. Ditto HEARTLAND. Bible Belt is not a new cocktail. It's a real force in the moral lives of millions of Americans. For top executives in the SOUTHLANDS, and those moving upwards in the organizations, drinking at noon, or in the evening, is not an everyday event. For every day, the ubiquitous glass of iced tea is at every hand. Business executives do drink at noon, on the right occasion. Male executives. There is an even stronger attitudinal resistance to females drinking in public than in other areas.

In spite of all, the average young SOUTHLANDS executive comes from one of the hardest drinking college backgrounds in America. Southern university undergraduates take pride in copious consumption of all alcoholic beverages, from wine to beer to moonshine, when they can get it. Boys and girls alike drink on a daily basis. There are some exceptions, but even many religiously supported institutions of higher learning have relaxed their once inviolate rules. Not all, but many. These two dichotomies—the sober, industrious manager and the heavy drinking college student—merge in a simple lifestyle. True to the Old South, when the SOUTHLANDS executive works, he or she "busts bunnies" (a regionalism) to do the job. Boozing at noon only slows afternoon efforts. When they play, however, booze is a crucial ingredient. And drinking is not only acceptable, but expected.

In HEARTLAND, there is, with alcohol as well as with all other activities except work and church, moderation. Few executives believe anyone is going straight to hell if his/her biggest sin is an occasional drink. But most hold, and will say so if pressed, that drinking is not "good." In other words, there is a mental bias against drinking as an act, based on a moralistic tradition. Come from outside HEARTLAND, order a Bloody Mary at noon, if you can find one, and you'll stand out from the crowd. They'll look, but never say a word. Just sip their iced tea and rattle ice cubes in the plastic glass.

NATURELAND and VASTLANDS folks imbibe. And do so in mixed company, although there is more male-alone executive drinking in VASTLANDS because there are more male executives. And males tend to drink more than females. At least they spend more time in bars.

Health interests of NATURELANDers dampen their volume, but not nearly as much as one might expect. It does bring them to beer and wine more than hard stuff, so they match national trends.

Beer is big in the VASTLANDS, too. But clear liquors—tequila, rum, and vodka in particular—are heavy sellers. Those who have the amber whiskey habit, maintain it.

A drink during a business lunch occurs frequently enough as to cause no notice. Executives follow the lead, as they do most places, of their superiors. If the boss has a pop, the rest can or cannot as they choose. Having two isn't a problem.

If you're from out of the region, watch it in the VAST-LANDS at night. VASTLANDers have been known to lift a few during a business meeting. Remember, they expect you to be up, bright-eyed and bushy-tailed, at an early hour in the A.M. They will be. Male and female alike. Control consumption accordingly. Each thousand feet of altitude gives every drink additional wallop.

Drinking during the business day in MEXICA? Why not? Who bothers over such issues? It's a little sticky with one woman present in a group of men. She can drink and no one will comment, but again, no one would be surprised, or upset, if she had iced tea. Sparkling waters have only invaded the big cities here, as in HEARTLAND. Outside urban centers, tall glasses of tea, at least half ice and rendered sickeningly sweet, are the rule.

WONDERLAND may have been the point of origin for the light movement. WONDERLANDers, in any case, have moved that way with dispatch. White wine has all but replaced vodka and is itself being ousted by sparkling waters. Alcohol is still consumed, but it is far more chic to teetotal than tipple. No one will notice if you order an alcoholic beverage or not. As long as you have something in hand or at your side which looks like a drink of some kind. Not drinking anything makes a WONDERLANDer nervous.

In summary, drinking isn't the business pastime it once was. Especially among under-thirty managers. The thirty-to-forty group is feeling a change. Over-forties continue pretty much as they have in the past, but consume less.

Drinking during business hours in a public place, no matter how elegant the surroundings, is not considered quite "right" in many areas, including the SOUTHLANDS and HEARTLAND. Drinking in the sanctuary of a private club, especially among the older group, is more relaxed. Female executives seem to have dealt with the problem quite well. HEARTLANDS, SOUTHLANDS, and MEXICA still exhibit some difficulty with this, but nothing sufficient to keep a lady from having a cocktail.

The three-martini lunch, as a daily affair, has had its day. If it ever was widely enjoyed after the close of the decade of the '60s.

FRATERNAL AND SERVICE CLUBS:

Another striking dissimilarity in executive behavior is seen in regional attitudes toward social/service/fraternal clubs and organizations. Rotary, Kiwanis, Odd Fellows, Moose, Mason, Optimist, and a dozen more similar names indicate organizations for male business executives and professionals. Females are forced to their own groups, usually allied with their business or profession.

Professional organizations for women are important and provide ample opportunity for networking. But they are completely different from the men-only social/civic/service clubs and fraternal orders. There are moves afoot to open some of these groups to women, and much will be accomplished as times passes. The "Ladies Auxiliary" adjunct groups, which for years were capable of taking care of members' wives while the men went off to conduct serious business, are not acceptable alternatives for today's female executives, or satisfactory to many members, either.

Men's civic, service, and social clubs show varying degrees of strength in different geographic areas. Most of these groups combine their meeting with lunch, are part business, part social, and each week present a program or speaker of interest (it is hoped) to its membership. Contacts are made, but little or no real business is discussed or transacted. Members are forced by rules to be earnestly concerned with their record of attendance, as excessive absences result in dismissal.

If you are visiting in a strong club region on Tuesday, Wednesday, or Thursday, popular days for gatherings, do not be surprised if you are asked to attend as a guest. It's an honor and a good way to get a sense of the community.

Again, rural-urban lines may be drawn to delineate popularity, but every huge city has several groups and usually some of the biggest names in business are long-time members. In smaller communities, belonging may be mandatory for any man who wishes to take an active role in community affairs. So it is common for large plant operations located near a small town to urge their executives to join and participate.

These organizations are most popular with business executives throughout the SOUTHLANDS, followed closely by HEARTLAND America. MEXICA falls third in this classification, followed by INDUSTRIA and the VASTLANDS. Remember, though, that every area of the U.S. has local chapters of these clubs, and members of the major organizations can be found across the nation. It's just that in the SOUTHLANDS, and to a slightly lesser degree in HEARTLAND, managers attach more importance to belonging. In these zones, higher ranking executives are more likely to be involved. If you are not from the SOUTHLANDS, be cautious about one habit. SOUTHLANDers will go to meetings religiously. Among themselves, they will speak in a somewhat disparaging manner about the organization, voicing complaints over the banality of programs, the food, or mandatory group singing. It is uncouth for an outsider to agree. More to the point, agreement will be taken as a personal affront. A vehement response is not an uncommon Southern reaction when an "outsider" criticizes a beloved institution.

SOCIAL CLUBS:

Managers have long practiced the art of clubsmanship. Although traditionally a man's prerogative, the burgeoning number of the female executives has placed a strain on the very existence of men-only social clubs. Fight as they might, sexual segregation in these bastions of prestige and privilege will come to an end. Not all are open to both sexes yet, and there may be a few holdouts that never will be. But the arrival of women in business surely spells the end of the all-male-club era.

Clubbiness is prevalent throughout American business. Upon rising to a certain position in management, the manager expects and is expected to take station in a club.

The country club is probably the most ubiquitous, even though the word "country" is a misnomer. Some of the most famous and revered are located within cities. A typical country club offers golf, tennis, a swimming pool, and entertainment/dining in a members-only facility. Variations on this theme include racquet clubs and swimming/tennis clubs, which are also popular. Membership in country clubs is consistent through all regions, although the number of clubs is lower in VASTLANDS.

There is an almost uncanny sameness to these institutions. The rusty statement, "If you've seen one, you've seen them all," is trusty, in this instance. Saturday night dances, Tuesday ladies luncheon groups, morning breakfast clubs, and a men's grill are all interchangeable modules without which the country club would not exist. Even the food, from roast beef to hamburgers, is nearly identical from Maine to California, and variations embracing regional cuisines are token.

Those parts of the CONSERVATORY under the influence of New York City exhibit country clubbiness on a grand scale. The SOUTHLANDS, too, place higher than normal value on country club membership.

The second most prevalent business-related club is the gentleman's club. Patterned after the English institution popular in London during the 1800s, and growing into a revered tradition, the club has several permutations.

At the top is the true club, owned and operated by the members, who hire professional management and an adequate staff. Facilities, almost always pre-World War II, and usually pre-1930s, house various dining rooms, a library, bars, a billiard parlor, and different athletic facilities complete with dressing and wet areas. Many also offer rooms and/or private quarters for entertaining. List these clubs and you have the crème de la crème of American clubbiness. Only a few cities have this type of institution and to call them exclusive is to misstate the situation. They are almost hereditary. Manhattan is a center for club-clubs, as is Boston.

Below this level are any number of lesser institutions that are still quite correct and more than sufficiently prestigious. These take various forms in different cities, but can be roughly classified as executive dining clubs. Most are sited near centers of business, most are actually luncheon clubs, and most experience highest member use rates between 11:00 A.M. and 2:00 P.M., Monday through Friday.

There are endless variations, from facilities owned by national companies in the business of providing this kind of club to members, to executive dining rooms owned by banks, insurance agencies, law firms, and others.

Such clubs exist in every major city and most smaller ones. To join is to be accepted into the business community, and in most places, all top management belongs to at least one.

Business discussed in the clubs is the business of the area and matches the makeup of the membership. Those who are artful (there seems to be little or no regional difference here) are able to play on their belonging to gain business for their firm or enhance their careers.

Clubsmanship, a male endeavor, may be on the wane, but from coast to coast, as more women become members, the club is ascendant. Variations are present, but nationally, membership is a surprisingly consistent management perk.

MONEY:

Let's talk about money. Money talk is difficult in some regions. Change that to a discussion of profits anticipated from a deal, and it's tougher still.

As any salesperson who calls on management will tell you, discussion of the cost of an item or service comes late in the presentation. First, because good salescraft dictates selling value before divulging price. Secondly, because, as odd as it seems, many executives become edgy discussing money. There are regional attitudes observable here, as there are in the subject of discussing profits.

Money, in the CONSERVATORY, is a sacred subject. As long as it is not easy to come by, and is earned, money is respectable. As an object of respect, it is spoken of reverently. And not spoken of too often, thank you very much. It is assumed all present in a business meeting can read a simple statement. Therefore, none should have any difficulty seeing for him/herself the anticipated profit from a new operation. The numbers are in place on the very thorough, very conservative pro forma. There is absolutely no need for anyone to speak those numbers aloud. Or (God forbid) in such WONDERLAND terms as "four million smackaroonies," or "four biggie big ones, which delivers one biggie big one for each of us."

If you're showing a deal in the CONSERVATORY, do exactly that. Show the deal. Figures on paper speak louder than words.

This is true if you're selling something, too. By mutual

agreement, discussion of price will be the last item of business. The seller desires this because that's the right order for a sales pitch; as does the CONSERVATORY buyer, because the rather distasteful discussion of price might be avoidable altogether if the product or total package is not precisely suitable for intended needs.

Since we mentioned WONDERLAND, it is only fitting to say that no discussion is complete without money figuring into it. In large amounts and talked about frequently. No inhibitions. If the seller doesn't bring up the cost of the offered item in the first few moments, the buyer will stop the sales presentation to ask. Without knowing the price, how can the buyer react to the sales presentation? Without knowing "how much," sales points have no meaning.

Discussion of profit in WONDERLAND is also vital in closing a deal. After all, there would be no reason for a deal if profits weren't to be made. That's a highly realistic viewpoint that can be carried to highly surrealistic levels, as seen by the absolute need not only to mention profits frequently, but also to almost gloat over the prospects. This is, after a fashion, a method of visualizing success which, psychologists assure us, is a viable procedure in goal attainment. So it is not just simple avarice. It is, however, one more example of flamboyant WONDERLAND behavior.

Profits are appreciated in the SOUTHLANDS, but mentioning them in business conversation, much less specifying an amount, is cretinous. Partners, in private, discuss such matters only when necessary. "Why talk about it?" is the attitude. "We all know we're in a deal to make money, but we're also here for each other and the fun of it. We don't discuss that side of business, either." Whether you accept this philosophy or not, if you do business south of the Mason-Dixon Divider, keep money talk to a minimum. Especially if you're selling something. No one will ask the price. Not if they're true SOUTHLANDers. They'll wait until you're done, then wait a little longer. The salesperson gives the cost once. There's no need to repeat it. Everyone present got the message.

One other SOUTHLANDS money quirk. Never alter an amount after it's presented. Once quoted, live with it. If you want to do another deal.

Money in INDUSTRIA is a tool. If you have a problem discussing a screwdriver or a milling machine, you'll have problems talking money with business executives in INDUS-TRIA. No need to be hesitant over prices or profits. Tools are worthless unless used. Executives intend to use money in INDUSTRIA because waste is abhorrent. Or possibly because money is like oil, and good machinery is kept well lubricated.

Money is a tool in the COMMERCIAL CORRIDOR, too. But here, there is a sharp definition between personal money and company money. Talk personal money, and all are silent. Talk corporate money and you can use amounts anytime you wish, as often as you wish. WONDERLAND overemphasis isn't advised, but there is no need for SOUTHLANDS silence, either. But do remember one thing. CORRIDOR folks are meeting aces. So get to the bottom line as quickly as possible, or your meeting to sell a new project may become a battleground between two other executives leaving you in the fire-controlled area.

Bottom-lining quickly is good for another reason, too. In the CORRIDOR, only the bottom line really counts. There's a lot of lip service to other facets of business, but the bottom line is where a CORRIDOR executive lives or dies.

In the rest of the nation, there isn't any special variation in money talk. They certainly don't mince numbers in Washington, D.C. And it's not against the code of MEXICA to haggle over price. The term "chisel," as used in "he kept chiseling me until I finally came down to three thou," is not positive. It is a negative word in MEXICA with a derogatory implication toward the one who "chiseled." It's okay in MEXICA to "negotiate" a price. But when either party goes after the last possible one-thousandth of a percent, it becomes chiseling. Both sides here like to "leave a little on the table," as they say, because it helps make everyone happy with the deal and the dealing. Both sides leave satisfied. "I could have gotten him to come down a little more, but what the hell. It's a fair price." "It was a tough deal and I could have held out for a little more, but what the hell, there's good profit in it." In MEXICA, enough, when dealing over money, seems to be enough. Or certainly sufficient. One who drives a hard bargain had best not drive too hard.

HANDSHAKES AND CONTRACTS:

All business executives are honorable; all men or women of their word. If they say they'll do something, you can be assured it will be done.

Everyone in American business would like to believe the above statement, but no one does. A modifier is necessary. People who do business in (insert name of your city or region here) are straight shooters. They give you their word, and one can bank it.

The modifier is, of course, your particular city or region. More than a little chauvinistic thinking is at work here. In many environs of the U.S., the above statement is both said and believed. In others, no one even bothers to say it because no one believes it.

Oil patch folks like to recall the many deals, involving millions if not billions of dollars, consummated with a handshake between two good old boys sitting on stools drinking coffee at the drugstore. They made a deal, shook hands, did the deal, and each one did what was right when called upon. That's the way the story goes. In reality, some deals were done that way. Others required a three-pound contract drawn up by twelve lawyers and a CPA who worked nights for a month to write it so even they couldn't understand it.

The "take-me-at-my-word, this-handshake-is-all-we'll-need,

let's-do-it" legend is offset by the "they-won't-pay-for-a-cup-of-coffee-unless-they-get-a-bill-of-sale-in-triplicate" school of thought. For most of America, business is conducted somewhere between the two. In a few areas, they go to extremes in one direction or the other.

Many forces are at play here. For instance, large, publicly held corporations cannot make handshake deals. Executives in these firms almost can't shake hands to symbolize their intent to review a matter further. Layers of management, approval requirements, and the ever-present possibility of an action being taken in direct violation of a previous agreement made years ago or in another country—all conspire to mandate hyper-thorough documentation of each transaction.

Size also plays an important role. Business people in small communities know each other personally and have a rather good idea of who can be trusted. Those in the oil exploration business during the 1950s and 1960s knew each other, too. There were only a limited number of players. Even when the field grew larger, if someone didn't know the newcomer, that someone knew someone who did. Small groups allow for effective censure. Ostracism is a strong incentive not to cheat; therefore, a major force in policing handshake deals.

Agreements made in or with firms in the COMMERCIAL CORRIDOR and INDUSTRIA, or in the cities of Atlanta, Chicago, or Los Angeles, require the highest level of paperwork. Do not be in a rush to close and get paid when dealing with these folks. Nothing will happen until it happens. And that will be when all documents are completed. Not a moment before.

Least deal documentation occurs in MEXICA, followed by the VASTLANDS, and dropping to a poor third, NATURELAND. They may not close any faster, for reasons discussed in an earlier chapter, but when the time comes, they will do so with less paperwork.

Supporters of stringent documentation insist their way will

hold future misunderstandings to a minimum. Lawsuits over disagreements concerning contractual agreements are more numerous in areas where large numbers of lawyers and large numbers of contracts are found. Please feel free to draw your own conclusions from this situation.

During earlier discussion of areas where the greatest amount of documentation is required to consummate an agreement, there is one omission. It was made on purpose because it sets a standard by which nothing may be judged. The sheer volume of paper needed to do a deal in Washington, D.C. far outstrips even the most flagrant demands of business elsewhere. There is no way to recount the documentation required to do business with the government. For those who do, paperwork is a substantial cost item carried, of course, into the price of goods and services being procured.

Just how far the paper situation in Washington has progressed can be seen from the fact that law firms, serving many government contractors who are toiling on classified projects, have CIA agents, who are also attorneys, on their staffs. Since the contracts are secret, but have to be drawn and discussed by legally knowledgeable individuals, the CIA lawyers receive necessary clearances and act on behalf of the law firms' clients, negotiating with similarly cleared federal attorneys. Washington, D.C. is a complex place, and doing business there is complicated. Many of those who are doing so successfully want to keep the complexity in place, to keep outsiders in their places.

IMAGES AND ROLES:

A potpourri wouldn't be complete without at least a mention of regional variations in self-image and role playing.

In some areas of the U.S., younger managers can claim a role by simply stating expertise in that field. In other words, he or she is what he/she claims to be because the claim makes it so. In other regions, no matter how much self-declamation is made, no one takes you for what you say but, rather, what you appear to be.

Confusing? You bet. Especially if you come from a "show me" country and run up against someone from a "say what I want to be" zone.

WONDERLAND is the toughest "show me" territory on earth. Probably because credits are so important. Recent credits, that is. It's not: "What have you done?", but "What have you done lately?" In the entertainment industry, and this transfers onto other business activities, one is only as good as his/her last performance. This attitude breeds an aggressive, almost hostile reaction to executive career claims.

"I'm an auditor," a simple statement, is met by "What have you audited lately?" There is constant demand for credits. Specific credits. Recent credits. One who claims to be proficient at something in WONDERLAND had best have proof of performance.

An executive would never claim to be expert or outstanding at anything in NATURELAND, the VASTLANDS, HEARTLAND, or MEXICA. In these territories, the most assertive personal aggrandizing statement would be, "Well, I know a little about that." This often will be followed by "Damn little, but some." In other words, personal accomplishment and career claims are underplayed, not boosted. One who overstates his/her ability will never be able to live up to the performance level required to maintain such an image. No one could. An individual who actually claimed to be a fast typist would have to be at least Olympic class, and that might not be enough. Even then, the person would still be considered boastful.

In the CONSERVATORY, claims are unnecessary. Everyone who is anyone knows everyone else, went to school with them, and is well acquainted with their ability as well as limitations. Naturally, newcomers find it troublesome to deal with this.

A SOUTHLANDer is careful of claims because boasting is seen as low, base behavior. This includes statements of personal ability. Claims will be more bountiful here than further west, but not so much as in the COMMERCIAL CORRIDOR.

The CORRIDOR, possibly because of crowded conditions, has its own criteria. "I'll take you for what you say you are, if you take me for what I say I am." It's a Golden Rule-do-unto-others situation that works because of mutual advantage. If someone asks if you can perform a certain task, and you want to do it, the proper CORRIDOR response is a flow of assuring positives.

Example:

"Hey, Charlie. Know anything about this tax matter?"

If Charlie wishes to respond in the affirmative, he will not use the "Well, a little" shy western response. He will immediately say, "Taxes? I know all about taxes. What kind of taxes? You came to the right person. I'm an expert." This might be followed by an anecdote dealing with a power figure who received aid from Charlie on a tax matter. The summation will reveal that Charlie is a long lost H&R Block family member.

A Westerner visiting the COMMERCIAL CORRIDOR would do well to remember that a string of self-spoken superlatives concerning the ability of an executive on any matter must be taken as meaning "a little." It's not braggadocio, it's CORRIDOR style.

The question of image and role playing in INDUSTRIA is an interesting one. If you ever desire to endure a dull, boring few minutes, ask for personal qualifications from an engineering type, or almost any upper echelon executive in this zone. No offense will be taken at your request. It's natural because any rational person would want to know. Plus, the code of factory/foundry management is, on this question, as intense as that of the Sicilian Omerta. And just as silent.

(For those not Mafia buffs, Omerta is that organization's rule
of silence. There ain't nobody who says nuthin' about nuthin'. No time. Not on your life.)

It would be an unthinkable breach of standards for an
INDUSTRIA executive to volunteer an in-depth background
profile. But the prepared executive is ever ready to unloose
a salvo of information once formally requested. At the end
of his/her monologue, you'll know more than you ever wanted.
Much more.

STATUS:

All America loves and craves status. Business executives from
one end of the U.S. to the other have, as a natural part of
their motivation, the promise of increased status, or the threat
of declining status.

Just as some individuals are more motivated by status
than others, some parts of the nation are more status oriented than others.

A case may be made for the SOUTHLANDS, where status is traditional and may or may not have as much to do
with money as whose family settled where first. Or founded
which bank when. The Principle of Inherited Merit domi-
nates, as evidenced by such remarks as "He has a wonderful
career behind him." It's hard to demonstrate status of that
category. It can't be worn or publicly displayed. People just
have to know, which may be the ultimate status of all.

Macho is a type of status. It comes from within, and while
it is present in everyone, males and females alike, it must
be nurtured in a certain way to blossom to status class. The
right level of macho can produce a status equal to that attained by conspicuous display of material riches. Why not,
as macho is a conspicuous display of a personal value system.

Status in HEARTLAND may take the form of acres owned
or acreage farmed or other land-agrarian pursuit. Size almost

always occurs in this region as part of the status symbol. That's why there are large banks, insurance companies, publicly owned utilities, and other significantly sized organizations. Given the choice of working for a large company or a small one, the prestige of a larger firm has effect here.

One assumes status in the VASTLANDS through self-belief. "I'm as 'who' as anyone" is a beginning self-realization statement. "Maybe even who-er" is graduate level.

Status plays a role in other areas as well, but for American Championship Status, the two ultimate centers are on opposite coasts. They balance each other like a huge dumbbell.

"Status and Status. Then more status. That's the name of the game." A quote from a New York City executive who lives in Manhattan. He is not, as he so quaintly put it, a "member of the bridge and tunnel crowd." That is to say, those individuals insufficiently fortunate as to have a stellar address in Manhattan and so must travel into the city (via bridges and tunnels) from outlying places with lower rents. Arguments will be raised over living in Manhattan or not. These usually concern family life and environment, valid points for many executives. But if you want big status, Manhattan is the place. Have a home in the country, too, if you like. But if you like status, at least one bedroom in midtown Manhattan is mandatory.

In some sections of New York City, status is more important than money. In all fairness, though, there is a great coming together of the two. It is impossible to attain or maintain status without having money to spend and be seen spending it. Dropping a bundle every night will not assure you of status, but not being able to drop a bundle every night will guarantee lack of same. There is no substitute in the New York prestige race for square green dollars (francs, lire, drachma, pounds, or you name it, as long as it's some nation's legal tender). Good job, great car, superb apartment, phenomenal contacts—these are all vital, but not worth nearly so much without ready cash. (Then again, probably not attainable or maintainable without a steady flow of bucks.)

Ready for the balancing act?

"Status out here is vital to any career. It's a matter of who you know and what you've done." A quote from a WONDERLANDer who has, by the by, ample status.

"New York status doesn't transfer. Money transfers well, but somehow, status stays behind. Except in rare cases." Another WONDERLAND wonderful.

If you want status on the Left Hand Coast, you have to be there to build it. Your tools will be a car, a beach house, a wardrobe, and at least a few contacts. The glue that holds it in place is money.

Given all the above, will you have status? Yes and no. More than the mere material items would acquire for you in Manhattan, but not to the maximum degree. What's the missing item? What you have done lately. Goal oriented, the WONDERLANDers. And they extend status to someone who has a box office hit, or develops a new computer process, or wins a huge contract, or helps put on the Olympics, or any of a multitude of other Aegean Stables type tasks.

Status for demonstrated success comes fast. It can arrive before the honoree has time to lease the car, rent the wardrobe, and move into the house. It has even been known to arrive before the notable receives his/her first check as compensation for the success. People here understand it takes time for the money to come in. After all, they wait until the last second before parting with theirs. (A promise that the check is in the mail is as false as a Palm Springs whore's protestations of unending love.) Money does come from success in WONDERLAND, though, and everybody knows it. The elite get to show their democratic ways by honoring the new status champ while he or she is still living poor.

There are similarities in New York and WONDERLAND

status, but though they are not very different, they aren't the same. WONDERLAND status seems to travel better because it arrives in Manhattan unscathed and mostly intact. New York status is a rather rara avis and doesn't have the wings to make it all the way West.

What is the highest status in the nation? Make it at both ends of the dumbbell, so there is equal stroke in Manhattan and WONDERLAND. Gain status on both coasts, and don't worry. They'll know who you are in Dubuque.

CHANGING REGIONAL BIAS:

Regional bias in the manners and behavior of business executives is not a stagnant condition. Changes come slowly because human attitudes are being dealt with, but changes nevertheless do come. A few examples will illustrate.

First, regional bias is growing stronger in MEXICA. This, after a major change in the attitudes of the area which took place between 1920 and 1960. During those years, Mexican-based culture established itself and kept unto itself, resisting change that always comes to subculture; and slowly, through population increases and improvement of economic conditions in the Latin community, made itself felt. This process is continuing. Examples are seen in legal requirements for bilingual announcements of governmental matters and public education of children from families that illegally entered the United States.

Business customs are reflecting this altered state of awareness. What is driving the new attitude toward even more acceptance? An older attitude, which holds that Latins must conform to Anglo values, is dying. As this recedes, the new MEXICA style rushes into fertile ground. The crest of the wave is not yet in sight. The pace of acceptance is accelerating, though, and shows every indication of becoming a force sufficiently strong to alter forever the region's bias.

WONDERLAND is another area where regional differentiation, especially in the business community, is increasing. State laws affecting business continue to reflect more and more protection for consumers and rejection of processes harmful to the environment. For years, Detroit has had to build special automobiles with altered safety and pollution control equipment just for this market. Manufacturers of other products are forced to follow. It is hard to imagine an area with such a completely different style from the balance of the U.S. becoming increasingly more different, but here it is. Remember, too, that some WONDERLAND style rubs off on us all, and as it does, seems less remote and bizarre. But having had what we are now only sampling as a base for future growth, business executives here are going to become increasingly different in more and more ways.

Regional business differentiation is weakening in the SOUTHLANDS. SOUTHLANDers please pardon this statement, but it's true. This continues a trend obvious in the general population for decades. Rebel yells and flags still receive homage, and the Confederate anthem, Dixie, continues to raise the hair on the back of every true Southerner's neck, but fewer of those necks are red. In-migration from the country to the city starts the process. The in-migration of industry and management from above the Mason-Dixon mixes population even further. Atlanta is a stronghold of aliens. Richmond is an outpost of Washington, D.C., in many ways. Other cities are also becoming more cosmopolitan.

That age-old prophecy "The South's gonna rise again!" is coming true. Just don't "Save your Confederate money, boys," another old slogan. "It ain't," in SOUTHLANDS vernacular, "gonna be worth a peck a dawg turds." The new SOUTHLANDS is going to be more like other American areas. Especially for executives doing business.

It's rather sad to see old ways fade. But then again, nostalgia is the protector of the inefficient. And more than enough

time has passed to heal wounds inflicted over a century and
a quarter ago.

FEDERAL ISSUES:

One last potpourri point. It deals with the business community and government. Both local and federal, but more federal, because the feds are not "on the ground" in every region of the U.S.

Actually, that statement, as a matter of strict fact, is not
correct. There is one branch of the federal government which
has full-time, paid staffers in virtually every county of America. Want to guess which Secretary's bailiwick this nationwide network falls under? If you guessed Agriculture, you
got it. County agents, trained agriculturists offering a service
to all residents in the form of counseling, testing, and instruction, have been with us since the 1930s. The program
is undergoing change at this time, but remains the most
widespread arm of the federals.

Overall, though, the Federal government is not standing
in D.C. with extended tentacles into every community. So
many regional attitudes, including those espoused by business executives, are missed. Not by the elected few, but by
the bureaucratic many.

Why is this important? Because regional bias among the
business community extends to different ideas and notions
about federal issues.

Take the use of arms and armed force to handle diplo-
matic difficulties through confrontation. MEXICA, HEART-
LAND, and the VASTLANDS are aviaries for Hawks. Business executives' support for aggressive military action, and,
therefore, a strong military with big budgets for defense, is
a given.

The business community in NATURELAND, because of
its interest in government defense contracts, goes along with

the massive military budget thrust, as does INDUSTRIA, but they do it for economic reasons. MEXICA, HEART-LAND, and VASTLANDS executives want to use, given proper motivation, military capabilities bought with those defense dollars. There is never, of course, one hundred percent agreement on any attitudinal issue, and especially not one as complex as the question of armed intrusion and combat as a means to settle disputes. Voices of peace ring through the three hawk nests. But the business community here has a much greater percentage of its members able to hark the cry of war birds while remaining deaf to the dove's soft coo.

SOUTHLANDers join their brethren to the west, but are more circumspect, serving as a sort of swing area between the aggressive West and the less pugnacious CONSERVA-TORY and COMMERCIAL CORRIDOR.

Powerful corollary viewpoint: If one is for constantly enhanced military capabilities, and therefore in favor of huge financial allocations in the Federal budget for "defense" purposes, one knows this can only happen if there is a corresponding decrease in social services and welfare expenditures.

In MEXICA, the VASTLANDS, and HEARTLAND, the tradition is for each man and woman to care for him/herself and family. In fact, this belief is sufficiently strong as to attach a stigma to those unable to cope. The attitude is so entrenched that any governmental meddling at any level, be it state, city, county, or Federal, is an intrusion on the rights of individual family members. The prevalent attitude is clear. A man—and women are included in this statement—ought to care for his family, help his friend, be ready to protect his country, and mind his own business. There's little room for government in that simplistic, four-point philosophy.

This is not to imply social programs are not popular in these zones. In many places, especially MEXICA, they accomplish a great deal. There is, though, a strong negative feeling toward taking "charity," and a full willingness to stifle funds for welfare or social action and give dollars to defense. Again, this is a broadly general statement that draws numerous dissenters. But it is a prevalent belief among management.

Contrast this again to strong support for welfare and social services from the CONSERVATORY and COMMERCIAL CORRIDOR. This also fits with prevailing views on defense allocations.

Taxation is another governmental function that meets with mixed feelings in the various regions' business communities.

Areas undergoing rapid population expansion, as those in MEXICA and the SOUTHLANDS, enjoy rising tax revenues, so managers here are more concerned with lessened Federal intervention in their affairs than with the burden of Federal taxation. This is enhanced by generally lower levels of tax imposed by city, state, and county governments, and the willingness of local and state authorities to favor programs and tax attitudes that enhance growth.

Other areas—the CONSERVATORY and COMMERCIAL CORRIDOR stand out as two examples—are not in a condition of uninhibited expansion and in-migration. Local and state revenue measures, to keep pace with public demand, exercise what many managers feel is a strain on commercial growth. The added burden of Federal tax is more noticeable under these conditions, so resistance to Federal levies is stronger here. Other reasons enter the picture, but overall, executives in these two areas are more resistant to taxes than those in MEXICA and SOUTHLANDS.

Several other Federal issues find differing response from business communities in the various regions, including, as might be expected, those dealing with environmental protection, agriculture, and energy. These regional differentiations are not as well known to many politicians and bureaucrats as they should be. More attention to them would result in improved governmental operations at the Federal level.

LE ENVOI:

Thank you for taking this casual cruise through the board-rooms and executive offices of America. If anyone has missed being offended, the omission is unintentional and apologies are respectfully offered.

Do not be misled by the banter and chiding in this tome. Truth will out and truth abounds in these many pages.

Use your new understanding as the basis for further observation. Above all, have fun with your hard-gained information. There is a place for more fun in every business.

It has been interesting being your tour guide on this invigorating outing. Thank you for the privilege.

INDEX